Ambrose / Harris

GRIDS

n. a structure or pattern
of lines used to guide the
placement of the elements
of a design

An AVA Book
Published by AVA Publishing SA
Rue des Fontenailles 16
Case Postale
1000 Lausanne 6
Switzerland
Tel: +41 786 005 109 Email: enquiries@avabooks.ch

Distributed by Thames and Hudson (ex-North America)
181a High Holborn, London WC1V 7QX, United Kingdom
Tel: +44 20 7845 5000 Fax: +44 20 7845 5055
Email: sales@thameshudson.co.uk
www.thamesandhudson.com

Distributed in the USA and Canada by:
Watson-Guptill Publications
770 Broadway
New York, New York 10003
Fax: +1 646 654 5487
Email: info@watsonguptill.com
www.watsonguptill.com

English Language Support Office
AVA Publishing (UK) Ltd.
Tel: +44 1903 204 455
Email: enquiries@avabooks.co.uk

ISBN 2-940373-77-9 and 978-2-940373-77-2
10 9 8 7 6 5 4 3 2 1

Design and text by Gavin Ambrose and Paul Harris
Original photography by Xavier Young
www.xavieryoung.co.uk

Production by AVA Book Production Pte. Ltd., Singapore
Tel: +65 6334 8173 Fax: +65 6259 9830 Email: production@avabooks.com.sg

Grids

Client: River Island
Design: Third Eye Design
Grid properties: The grid helps to position elements and develop flow within the page

River Island

This is a spread from a catalogue created by Third Eye Design for fashion retailer River Island. It features a combination of modules, columns, text and images to establish a narrative. The grid offers a structure that guides the placement of the different design elements. It directs the reader's attention around the spread, following a continuous and logical flow.

Contents

Webb & Webb

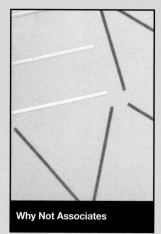

Why Not Associates

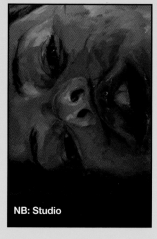

NB: Studio

3 Deep Design

Third Eye Design

The Vast Agency

Introduction

A grid is the foundation upon which a design is constructed. It allows the designer to effectively organise various elements on a page. In essence, it is the skeletal structure of a piece of work. Grids bring order and structure to designs, whether they are as simple as the one pictured opposite, or as heavily populated as those on newspaper websites.

This book aims to introduce the basic principles of grid usage in graphic design as practised by contemporary designers. Many of these fundamentals date back centuries to when books first started to be mass produced. However, these methods have been refined, improved and complemented throughout the ages. This process continues as new technology brings forth new media such as Internet pages and mobile telephones.

However, the book is not intended to be a prescriptive guide to setting up and using grids. Instead, it will look at the principles behind grid usage in order to give the reader the ability to tackle a wide variety of graphic design problems. The book's main message is that a static and repetitive approach to grid use does not result in effective and creative designs. By developing a clear understanding of the many facets of the grid, we hope to prove that grids not only bring order to a design, but also provide ample opportunities for expression and creativity.

The need for grids
Grids are necessary guides that provide order to the elements of a design, helping readers to access information easily.

Grid basics
This section is an introduction to the elements that make up a grid, which includes measurements, shapes, proportions and various rules relating to the anatomy of a page.

Grid types
This chapter shows the relationships between grids, typography and images by exploring and presenting some of the many different grid types available.

Grid elements
The grid is used to position the various picture, text and graphic elements comprising a design to produce different visual presentations.

Grid usage
Here, different grids and techniques are discussed to provide a guide for structuring and presenting different types of content including the use of orientation, juxtaposition and space division.

Grids on the Web
This chapter covers special design considerations for producing grids and layouts for Web pages and other electronic media.

Client: Nike
Design: Why Not Associates
Grid properties: Footwear illustrations are aligned in columns and rows, providing clean lines and order

Nike Paris
This retail interior was created by Why Not Associates for the Nike store on the Champs-Elysées in Paris. It features a repeated pattern of sports shoe illustrations on the interior glass walls, which are aligned in columns (vertical) and rows (horizontal). This wall conveys the message that a grid structure is present in many of the things we see every day.

This book introduces different aspects of grid usage via dedicated chapters for each topic. Each chapter provides numerous examples showing unique and creative grid use in the work of leading contemporary design studios, which are annotated to explain the reasons behind the design choices made.

Key design principles are isolated so that the reader can see how they are applied in practice.

Clear navigation
Each chapter has a clear strapline, which allows readers to quickly locate areas of interest.

Introductions
Special section introductions outline basic concepts that will be discussed.

Organising information

12 13

Organising information
The basic function of a grid is to organise the information on a page. The way this is achieved has been developed and refined throughout history – from simple pages of text, to the incorporation of images and to the diverse possibilities provided by modern design software.

Although the grid has developed considerably over time, the basic principles underpinning it have remained intact for centuries. Approximately 300 years separate the two images on this page, but the common elements between them are clearly seen. The page from the medieval manuscript (below left) and the newspaper (below right) both have columns that contain and shape the body text into a readable measure. The titling provides clarity and a basic hierarchy.

Pictured far left is an early Latin printed page, incunabula, dated 1483, with text in two vertical columns, and an early newspaper (left), the Edinburgh Evening Courant from 1774, which features three text columns. Both have common elements that guide the reader: clear headers and a sense of direction. In the latter example, additional elements such as drop capitals and scotch rules add to the sense of order.

Hierarchy
A logical, organised and visual guide for text that indicates different levels of importance.

Scotch rules
A thick, thin or thin-thick combination of lines used to separate different text elements.

Jan Samsom
This poster was created by Faydherbe / De Vringer for a Jan Samsom exhibit. The design features an intuitive grid that gives a centralised and symmetrical structure to the text elements based around the central placement of the word 'Samsom', which then acts as a counterpoint to the asymmetrical image.

The design features a clear and unambiguous hierarchy of information, while being typographically diverse and dynamic. Text columns run both horizontally and vertically, adding a sense of layering. The information appears set in either the fore-, mid- or background, depending on its size and colour intensity.

Client: CBK
Ar-toteek Dordrecht
Design:
Faydherbe / De Vringer
Grid properties: Symmetrical and central grids, combined with an asymmetrical image.

Related information
Related information such as definitions are isolated and explained.

Examples
Commercial projects from contemporary studios and designers bring to life the principles under discussion.

Diagrams

Diagrams add meaning to theory by showing the basic principles in action.

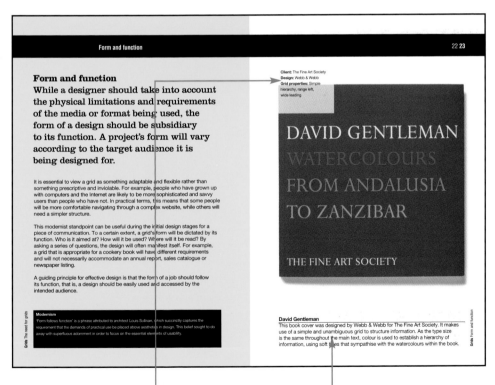

Additional information

Clients, designers and grid usage principles are included.

Written explanations

Key points are explained within the context of an example project.

Client: University of the Arts, London

Design: Research Studios

Grid properties: Symmetrical two-column grid with wide scholars margins

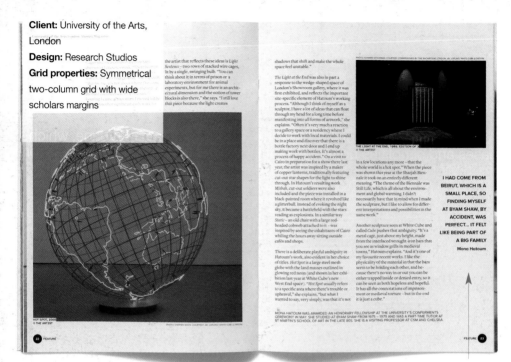

Spread A (top)

the artist that reflects these ideas is *Light Sentence* – two rows of stacked wire cages, lit by a single, swinging bulb. "You can think about it in terms of prison or a laboratory environment for animal experiments, but for me there is an architectural dimension and the notion of tower blocks is also there," she says. "I still love that piece because the light creates

shadows that shift and make the whole space feel unstable."

The Light at the End was also in part a response to the wedge-shaped space of London's Showroom gallery, where it was first exhibited, and reflects the important site-specific element of Hatoum's working process. "Although I think of myself as a sculptor, I have a lot of ideas that can float through my head for a long time before manifesting into all forms of artwork," she explains. "Often it's very much a reaction to a gallery space or a residency where I decide to work with local materials. I could be in a place and discover that there is a bottle factory next door and I end up making work with bottles. It's almost a process of happy accident." On a visit to Cairo in preparation for a show there last year, the artist was inspired by a maker of copper lanterns, traditionally featuring cut-out star shapes for the light to shine through. In Hatoum's resulting work *Misbah*, cut-out soldiers were also included and the piece was installed in a black-painted room where it revolved like a glitterball. Instead of evoking the night sky, it became a battlefield with the stars reading as explosions. In a similar way *Static* – an odd chair with a large red-beaded cobweb attached to it – was inspired by seeing the inhabitants of Cairo whiling the hours away sitting outside cafes and shops.

There is a deliberate playful ambiguity in Hatoum's work, also evident in her choice of titles. *Hot Spot* is a large steel mesh globe with the land masses outlined in glowing red neon (and shown in her exhibition last year at White Cube's new West End space). "*Hot Spot* usually refers to a specific area where there's trouble or upheaval," she explains, "but what I wanted to say, very simply, was that it's not

in a few locations any more – that the whole world is a hot spot." When the piece was shown this year at the Sharjah Biennale it took on an entirely different meaning. "The theme of the Biennale was Still Life, which is all about the environment and global warming. I didn't necessarily have that in mind when I made the sculpture, but I like to allow for different interpretations and possibilities in the same work."

Another sculpture seen at White Cube and called *Cube* pushes that ambiguity. "It's a metal cage, just above my height, made from the interlaced wrought-iron bars that you see as window grills in medieval towns," Hatoum explains. "And it's one of my favourite recent works. I like the physicality of the material in that the bars seem to be holding each other, and because there's no way in or out you can be either trapped inside or denied entry, so it can be seen as both hopeless and hopeful. It has all the connotations of imprisonment or medieval torture – but in the end it is just a cube."

> I HAD COME FROM BEIRUT, WHICH IS A SMALL PLACE, SO FINDING MYSELF AT BYAM SHAW, BY ACCIDENT, WAS PERFECT... IT FELT LIKE BEING PART OF A BIG FAMILY
> Mona Hatoum

THE LIGHT AT THE END, 1989, EDITION OF 3
© THE ARTIST

HOT SPOT, 2006
© THE ARTIST
PHOTO: STEPHEN WHITE. COURTESY JAY JOPLING/WHITE CUBE (LONDON)

MONA HATOUM WAS AWARDED AN HONORARY FELLOWSHIP AT THE UNIVERSITY'S CONFERMENTS CEREMONY IN MAY. SHE STUDIED AT BYAM SHAW FROM 1975 – 1979 AND WAS A PART-TIME TUTOR AT ST MARTIN'S SCHOOL OF ART IN THE LATE 80S. SHE IS A VISITING PROFESSOR AT CSM AND CHELSEA.

A

Spread B (bottom)

Mona Hatoum

WORDS~HELEN SUMPTER

MONA HATOUM'S biography is well documented. Born in Beirut in 1952 to Palestinian parents she studied and has lived in London since the mid-1970s after she was prevented from returning home from a visit to London when civil war broke out in the Lebanon. Since then she has become internationally renowned for her early performance works in the mid-1980s exploring issues of politics and gender, and her later sculptural works and large-scale sculptural installations that deal with themes of incarceration, surveillance, borders and boundaries and the problematic relationship of domestic objects rendered potentially dangerous. Her international reputation has resulted in participation in major exhibitions, including the Venice Biennale and Documenta, and she was nominated for the Turner Prize in 1995.

Among her early signature works is *The Light at the End* (1989) a narrowing corridor ending in a gate of vertical heating element bars. It's a work that still resonates for the artist today. "When I moved out of performance and got into installation, I wanted the work to have a less direct message and be more about a general feeling of insecurity or danger or of an object alienated from its normal use," Hatoum explains. "*The Light at the End* was the first work I made that I felt created that feeling and worked on several levels – physical, intellectual and emotional. It's quite reduced and minimal but it reverberates with meanings of imprisonment, torture and pain. And I like the ambiguity; not only do you not know whether you are the jailer or jailed, inside or outside, but the title promises something positive and in the end it's burning hot and dangerous."

CUBE, 2006
© THE ARTIST
PHOTO: STEPHEN WHITE. COURTESY JAY JOPLING/WHITE CUBE (LONDON)

B

The need for grids

Before looking at grids in detail, this first chapter will look at the basic purpose of a grid and why they are used by graphic designers. Subsequent chapters will look at the placement of elements within a grid and how this impacts on the overall design.

A grid provides a structure for all the design elements of a page, which eases and simplifies both the creative and decision-making process for the designer. Using a grid allows for greater accuracy and consistency in the placement of page elements, providing a framework for a high degree of creativity. Grids allow a designer to make informed decisions and to use their time efficiently. They can be used to add a high degree of dynamism to a design – the positioning of what may seem a rather small and irrelevant element, such as a folio, can create a dramatic impact on a page, which pulses through a printed work.

Although many of us now view content in an electronic format or via the Web, the structural principles behind the designing of a printed page still apply since the way we read a page and how we extract information from it remains the same.

University of the Arts, London (left)

These two spreads are from the alumni magazine of the University of the Arts in London created by Research Studios. It uses a simple, symmetrical two-column grid with wide scholars margins (A), and a single text column on the opener pages (B). The scholars margin was originally used for notes and marginalia, and can be incorporated into a design as a block of white space. The design features a strong grid, with picture elements straddling columns to create a sense of movement. The folios, inserted as graphic elements in the fore-edge of the foot margin, offer a strong anchor to the design. The range of typefaces and sizes used for headers, body copy and captions creates a playful sense of typographic 'colour' (this is discussed further on page 84) and individuality.

Organising information

The basic function of a grid is to organise the information on a page. The way this is achieved has been developed and refined throughout history – from simple pages of text, to the incorporation of images and to the diverse possibilities provided by modern design software.

Although the grid has developed considerably over time, the basic principles underpinning it have remained intact for centuries. Approximately 300 years separate the two images on this page, but the common elements between them are clearly seen. The page from the medieval manuscript (below left) and the newspaper (below right) both have columns that contain and shape the body text into a readable measure. The titling provides clarity and a basic hierarchy.

Pictured far left is an early Latin printed page, *incunabula*, dated 1483, with text in two vertical columns, and an early newspaper (left), the *Edinburgh Evening Courant* from 1774, which features three text columns. Both have common elements that guide the reader: clear headers and a sense of direction. In the latter example, additional elements such as drop capitals and scotch rules add to the sense of order.

Hierarchy

A logical, organised and visual guide for text that indicates different levels of importance.

Scotch rules

A thick, thin or thin-thick combination of lines used to separate different text elements.

Client: CBK
Artoteek Dordrecht
Design:
Faydherbe / De Vringer
Grid properties: Symmetrical and central grids, combined with an asymmetrical image

Jan Samsom

This poster was created by Faydherbe / De Vringer for a Jan Samsom exhibit. The design features an intuitive grid that gives a centralised and symmetrical structure to the text elements based around the central placement of the word 'Samsom', which then acts as a counterpoint to the asymmetrical image.

The design features a clear and unambiguous hierarchy of information, while being typographically diverse and dynamic. Text columns run both horizontally and vertically, adding a sense of layering. The information appears set in either the fore-, mid- or background, depending on its size and colour intensity.

Grids Organising information

How we read a page

Any given page will feature active and passive areas due to the nature of the content and the way an individual views a page – how the eye naturally scans a page to locate information.

The active and passive areas of design

A designer has a great deal of freedom in placing different design elements within a layout. However, the way in which the human eye scans an image or a body of text means that certain areas of a page are 'hotter' or more active than others. This means that central and peripheral areas exist within a page. Designers can use this knowledge to direct the placement of key design elements – either making them more prominent or less noticeable.

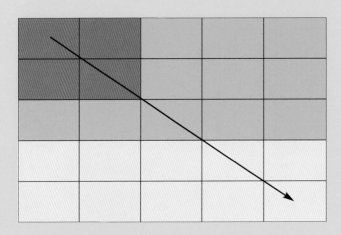

When faced with a new page of information, the human eye habitually looks for an entrance at the top left and scans down and across to the bottom right corner, as shown in the illustration. The depth of the colours indicates where the strongest focus of attention is.

The Arts and Crafts Movement (right)

These two spreads are from a book about the Arts and Crafts Movement created by Webb & Webb. It features colour images in the principal hotspot at the top, left-hand corner of the page. The use of images excites the eye with a burst of colour and draws the viewer into the spreads. The placement of both text and image elements on the grid adds a subtle movement to the spreads without creating confusion and inhibiting reading. In this instance the grid 'contains' the elements without stifling them.

Client: Phaidon
Design: Webb & Webb
Grid properties: Colour images in the grid are located in the main page hotspot

CRAFT AND COMRADESHIP IN THE ARTS AND CRAFTS

IN THE 1860s AND 1870s THE ARTS AND CRAFTS HAD BEEN CHARACTERIZED BY AN INTERLACING WEB OF THEMES. IN THE 1880s AND 1890s, HOWEVER, ONE STRAND CAME TO THE FORE – THAT OF FELLOWSHIP.

This was linked to the rise of socialism, with its agenda of shifting systems of power and means of production from private hands to the community as a whole. Many members of the Arts and Crafts Movement in Britain became committed socialists, its byword of social inclusion matching their concern to democratize the arts. Fellowship as a form of empowerment also developed in other walks of life, from welfare and science to education and philanthropy, and while some of the groups which resulted were little more than clubs for hard drinking and glutinous dining, others, such as the Institution of Civil Engineers, were committed to a specific cause. There was a rise in the membership of friendly societies, a network of working-class clubs which stemmed from trade-related associations of the eighteenth century, and offered subsidies such as sickness and funeral benefit (by 1880, membership had reached approximately 5.5 million). From the middle of the century trade unionism was also on the increase, and in 1889 the Fabian Society was established with the aim of engaging in non-revolutionary reform along socialist lines. On a less political level, there was everything from the literary and philosophical societies, which increased rapidly from the 1820s, to the intriguing Society for the Suppression of Vice.

Whatever their size or purpose, these groups all shared a fundamental sense of community. This had featured strongly in the rhetoric of Pugin, Ruskin and Morris, and in the 1880s was to become a defining characteristic of the British Arts and Crafts Movement. As Morris insisted in his socialist story, *A Dream of John Ball*, which was published in instalments from 1886 to 1887: 'Fellowship is heaven, and lack of fellowship is hell; fellowship is life, and lack of fellowship is death.' Reflecting this sentiment, a succession of craft guilds, workshops and societies began to develop throughout Britain, its city centres and rural retreats, with formal manifestos or simple bonds of friendship, each realizing to varying degrees the social, creative and, on occasion, philanthropic aims of the Arts and Crafts. If, up until now, the Movement had been a set of ideas and aspirations shared by a few unsettled and charismatic individuals, in the 1880s it acquired a wide support base, a coherent identity and, in 1887, a name, when the writer and bookbinder Thomas James Cobden-Sanderson (1840–1922) coined the phrase 'the Arts and Crafts'.

Some of the earliest craft associations of the period were run by women, for whom the applied arts had long been an acceptable form of activity. In 1872 Elizabeth Wardle

53

THE ARTS AND CRAFTS MOVEMENT

commissioned the pair to design a music salon for his Viennese mansion earlier that year. Inspired by what they had seen, the two Austrians resolved 'to create an island of tranquillity in our own country, which, amid the joyful hum of arts and crafts, would be welcome to anyone who professes faith in Ruskin and Morris.' The result, the Wiener Werkstätte, opened in Vienna in 1903, financed by Wärndorfer and directed by Hoffmann and Moser. Hoffmann's friend from Secession days.

In the Wiener Werkstätte's first Work Programme of 1905 Hoffmann launched a splenetic invective against the trumpery of modern design: 'The boundless evil caused by shoddy mass-produced goods and by the uncritical imitation of earlier styles, is like a tidal wave sweeping across the world. [...] The machine has largely replaced the hand and the business-man has supplanted the craftsman.' To counteract this, the Werkstätte aimed to provide craftsmen with a forum in which to practise and publicize their skills, hoping in the process to re-establish the role of the craftsman in contemporary production, and to improve the standards and availability of good design. As Hoffmann explained, 'We wish to create an inner relationship linking public, designer and

worker and we want to produce good and simple articles of everyday use. Our guiding principle is function, utility our first condition, and our strength must lie in good proportions and the proper treatment of material.' True to his word, Hoffmann designed cutlery (fig. 157) which is proud, strong and devoid of fuss, with a minimum of joints and details which might be weakened or damaged by the wear and tear of everyday use. His silver sugar pot with a simple fruit motif (fig. 158), on the other hand, is a seductive exercise in truth to materials, its tactile curves exploring the silver's polished sheen. Moser too flaunted good materials and skilled craftsmanship in pieces such as his music cupboard (fig. 159), which was treated with white lead to enhance the natural grain of the oak. The stylized female figures on its chased silver plaques point to aesthetic considerations shared with the Glasgow Four, whose work was much admired in Vienna at the time.

The Wiener Werkstätte laid great emphasis on the well-being of its workers, even if this meant charging high prices. The inevitable result was that the Werkstätte found itself working for the moneyed elite and gradually moved into the luxury of Art Nouveau. In the Palais Stoclet (1905–11)

128

129

Client: Paris 2012
Olympic Committee
Design: Research Studios
Grid properties: Colour
hotspots are used to
draw attention

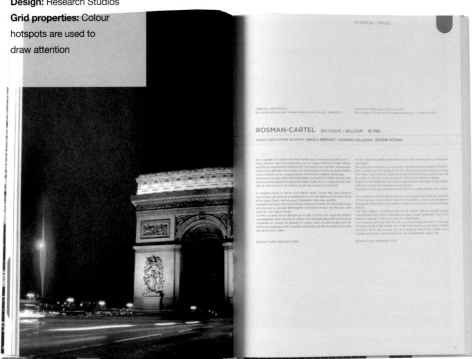

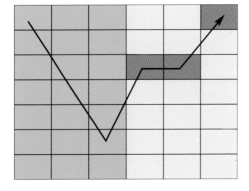

This illustration depicts the hotspots of the spread above. Notice how the title and folio have more pull than the image.

Paris 2012

This brochure was created by Research Studios for the 2012 Olympic architectural bids. It features the use of colour to create visual hotspots. While the full-bleed image may initially draw attention, the red titling and indicator mark grab the reader's attention as the eye naturally scans to the right and is then pulled to the text, as shown on the left. Notice how the text is roughly aligned to the form of the subject of the image, the Arc de Triomphe in Paris.

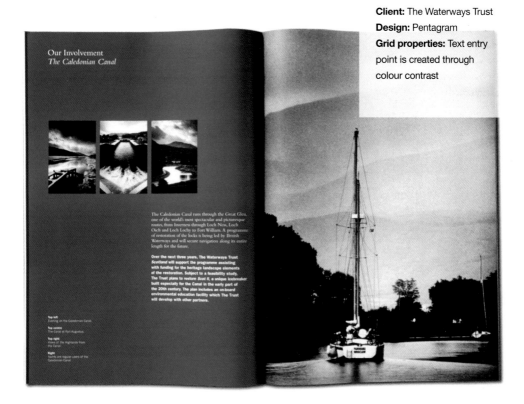

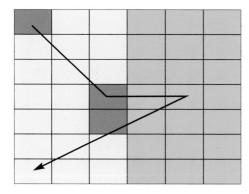

Client: The Waterways Trust

Design: Pentagram

Grid properties: Text entry point is created through colour contrast

This illustration shows that the white text sections reversed out of the blue verso page are the main hotspots on the spread above.

The Waterways Trust

Pentagram's brochure for The Waterways Trust uses white text against a dark background to form hotspots that serve as entry points for the eye, which mirrors the effect on the opposite page.

The page has a clear sense of 'flow' enforced by the grid structure – there is a clear pattern of movement from title, to image, to text and finally to caption.

How we view a screen

People scan Web pages in the same way that they scan a printed page to search for key words or things of interest. A designer can aid this process by highlighting keywords and using bullet points to ensure that the most important sections of information leap out.

F-Pattern for reading Web content

Research has shown that people tend to read Web pages in an F-shaped pattern, as shown in the illustration below. They quickly scan across the top from left to right in two stripes, and then scan down the page as they rapidly move forward in search of something meaningful. In terms of design, this means that key information and entry points should be located within the ambit of the F-Pattern to increase the chances of catching the reader's attention.

The top bar of the F-Pattern represents the viewer's initial left-to-right scan, which extends well across the page. A second scan lower down is more abrupt and forms the F's crossbar. Finally, the viewer quickly scans down the page, forming the F-Pattern's stem.

This is a general rule that can only be used as a guide. In practice, scanning pattern varies according to the design. A design with an element in a normally inactive area will elicit a different scan.

F-shaped reading pattern
Pattern resulting from the attempt to quickly draw information from a website.

DAN TOBIN SMITH
STILL LIFE
INTERIORS
LANDSCAPE
ADVERTISING

Client: Dan Tobin Smith
Design: Studio Output
Grid properties: Simple
navigation compatible with
the F-shaped scanning motion

ARCHIVE
CONTACT

DAN TOBIN SMITH
STILL LIFE
INTERIORS
LANDSCAPE
ADVERTISING

Fridge.
February 2005.

1

Magazine.
Kilimanjaro

ARCHIVE
CONTACT

Dan Tobin Smith

This is the website of photographer Dan Tobin Smith, which was designed by
Studio Output. The navigation is simple and effective as all the information is
compatibly laid out to the F-shaped reading pattern. The featured photographic
works are displayed as a series of thumbnails on a grid, which can be enlarged to

The inverted pyramid

The inverted pyramid style of presenting information is prevalent in newspaper journalism. The most important piece of information appears first while subsequent information decreases in importance. When applied to the screen, the grid and structure used vary from that of conventional print design due to the limited time a viewer spends on each page. As the viewer will not read all the text, the most important information has to lead, accompanied by clearly defined subheads on the left to fit with the F-viewing pattern.

It is also worth remembering that if the design relies on scrolling down beyond the 'fold' point, not all viewers will see the secondary content. For this reason, it is important that the design structure effectively uses and maximises the impact of the top portion of the grid.

The inverted pyramid

The inverted pyramid of information means that the most important and powerful information goes at the top, followed by secondary information, while more general information comes last.

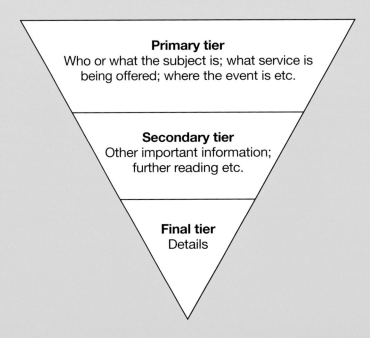

Primary tier
Who or what the subject is; what service is being offered; where the event is etc.

Secondary tier
Other important information; further reading etc.

Final tier
Details

Web page fold
The fold of a Web page is the imaginary line that limits what you can see before having to scroll down. The smaller the screen or the lower the screen resolution, the higher up the content fold will occur. Key information should be located above the fold to minimise the amount of searching viewers have to do.

F-scan start point

The general start point for a Web design. In this case, it features the company logo.

800 x 600 pixels

Apple's recommended minimum of 413 pixels down the grid would be the 'fold' point for an 800 x 600 screen. All navigation devices fall above this point.

THE
GEORGE
HOTEL
& Brasserie

the hotel
our rooms
book a room
food & drink
location & parking
hotel history
about cranbrook
site map
brochure request
contact

The interior design is a clever
and stylish contemporary dé...

Welcome to The George Hotel & Brasserie
The George Hotel & Brasserie is one of
Cranbrook's most historical landmark bu...
dating back to the 14th Century. It is now
transformed to one of the most unique b...
hotels in Kent with 12 individually design...
rooms offering a blend of period and
contemporary style. Both the awarded d...
room and brasserie offer a regularly cha...ging
menu using produce mainly sourced fro... the
Kent and Sussex countryside and coast

Whilst staying in Cranbrook you will be situated
in the heart of The Weald of Kent which is ideally
located for exploring Kent and Sussex and
seeking out the many attractions The Garden of
England has to offer such as Sissinghurst Castle
Gardens, Royal Tunbridge Wells and the historic
cinque ports of Tenterden and Rye.

Learn more in our hotel history section

Client: The George Hotel & Brasserie
Design: Gavin Ambrose
Grid properties: Top left entry point and the inverted pyramid hierarchy

1024 x 768 pixels

The 'fold' point on the most widely used screen size of 1024 x 768 is 581 pixels down the screen.

Our rooms
We want you to enjoy your stay at
The George Hotel which is why we
offer some of the most comfortable
hotel rooms in Cranbrook and indeed
Kent.

All of our rooms are individually
designed offering a unique choice of
period or contemporary style. With
sumptuous fabrics centred around
commissioned or discovered pieces
of furniture and art. They offer many
features to enhance your stay such
as the latest flat panel TV's with
SKY.

Book online

The George Hotel & Brasserie included in The Good Food Guide 2008
The George Hotel in Cranbrook, Kent is proud to have been included The
Good Food Guide 2008. This prestigious acknowledgement is awarded to no
more that 1200 UK restaurants out of some 30000 and sets us amongst
some of the finest restaurants in Kent and the U.K. Whether you are seeking
a hotel in Cranbrook or simply an excellent restaurant in Cranbrook the
George Hotel Brasserie will endeavour to remain at the forefront of dining in
Kent.

For further information on the guide, click here

The grid

The grid intentionally follows a 'magazine' format, with a series of image 'collections' and narrower column widths.

The finest freshest food in Kent
The George Hotel & Brasserie
creates a relaxed atmosphere in
which to enjoy first class cuisine
which has developed an excellent
reputation amongst restaurants in
Kent and Sussex and has won
country wide acclaim from industry
experts. The hotel is now recognised
for culinary excellence with an AA
rosette and is complimented by a well
selected wine list which scales the
globe from famous French wines to
the lesser known new world wines of
the southern hemisphere and wines
from our very own Garden of England
vineyards by Chapel Down in
Tenterden, Kent.

View our menu online

The George Hotel, Stone Street, Cranbrook, Kent TN17 3HE T.01580 713348 E.reservations@thegeorgehotelkent.co.uk

The George Hotel & Brasserie

This is the Web page for the George Hotel & Brasserie, which was created by Gavin Ambrose. It uses a grid structure compatible with the F-scan reading pattern, using a solid entry point at the top left corner – a menu reads down from this point and subheads then sprout from it. The page is designed like a magazine spread using the inverted pyramid hierarchy so that the most relevant and current information is placed at the top, while secondary information is presented below the fold or viewable area.

Form and function

While a designer should take into account the physical limitations and requirements of the media or format being used, the form of a design should be subsidiary to its function. A project's form will vary according to the target audience it is being designed for.

It is essential to view a grid as something adaptable and flexible rather than something prescriptive and inviolable. For example, people who have grown up with computers and the Internet are likely to be more sophisticated and savvy users than people who have not. In practical terms, this means that some people will be more comfortable navigating through a complex website, while others will need a simpler structure.

This modernist standpoint can be useful during the initial design stages for a piece of communication. To a certain extent, a grid's form will be dictated by its function. Who is it aimed at? How will it be used? Where will it be read? By asking a series of questions, the design will often manifest itself. For example, a grid that is appropriate for a cookery book will have different requirements and will not necessarily accommodate an annual report, sales catalogue or newspaper listing.

A guiding principle for effective design is that the form of a job should follow its function, that is, a design should be easily used and accessed by the intended audience.

Modernism

'Form follows function' is a phrase attributed to architect Louis Sullivan, which succinctly captures the requirement that the demands of practical use be placed above aesthetics in design. This belief sought to do away with superfluous adornment in order to focus on the essential elements of usability.

Client: The Fine Art Society
Design: Webb & Webb
Grid properties: Simple
hierarchy, range left,
wide leading

DAVID GENTLEMAN
WATERCOLOURS
FROM ANDALUSIA
TO ZANZIBAR

THE FINE ART SOCIETY

David Gentleman

This book cover was designed by Webb & Webb for The Fine Art Society. It makes use of a simple and unambiguous grid to structure information. As the type size is the same throughout the main text, colour is used to establish a hierarchy of information, using soft hues that sympathise with the watercolours within the book.

Client: Antique Collectors Club
Design: Webb & Webb
Grid properties: Simple grid prioritising image presentation

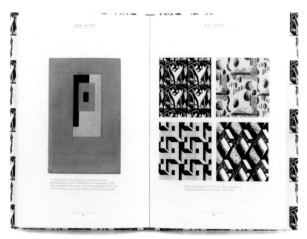

A grid has been used loosely for these spreads (top and bottom) to give prominence to the images.

Antique Collectors Club

These spreads are from a publication designed by Webb & Webb. It uses a simple grid that gives priority to the images. The form of the grid is dictated by its function: to focus on the images and give them sufficient space. The top spread features works by Edward Bawden and Eric Ravilious, while the bottom has works by Paul Nash and John Nash.

Client: Luke Hughes & Company
Design: Webb & Webb
Grid properties: Dynamic folio placement, and strong sense of product placement

Luke Hughes

This book on bespoke chairs was designed by Webb & Webb for Luke Hughes & Company. It features the dynamic placement of folios within red circles, which are then positioned on the outside edge of the pages. The central alignment of the red circles effectively draws attention, and their appearance on the recto pages prompts the reader to turn the page.

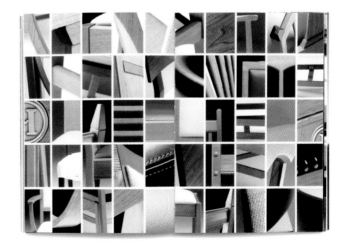

Images dominate these spreads and the bold placement of the folio (top) brings a sense of movement to the design. The grid is explicitly used (bottom) by showing a collage of details and demonstrating the quality of the product.

Client: NB: Studio
Design: NB: Studio
Grid properties: Loose grid formed by objects

Grid basics

A grid is the basic framework with which a design is created. It provides a reference structure that guides the placement of the elements forming the anatomy of a design such as text, images and illustrations, in addition to general elements such as straplines and folios.

Since a grid delineates the space on a page or spread, effective grid use requires an understanding of the absolute and relative measurements used to form it. The grid is not a prescriptive design tool, however, and there are various ways of using grids in order to produce a dynamic design. This may include the creation of active hotspots or shapes; using different proportions to add movement; or establishing a hierarchy.

NB: Studio (left)

The poster on the left was created by NB: Studio for a lecture by one of its designers, Daniel Lock. It features a loose grid composed of a collection of visitor badges. The badges display some of the studio's activities and clients, while the final pass in the grid at the bottom right-hand corner contains details about the lecture.

ISO and paper sizes

Standard paper sizes provide a means for designers, printers and others involved in the printing and publishing industries to communicate product specifications and control costs.

The ISO (International Organization for Standardization) paper sizing system is based on a height-to-width ratio of the square root of two (1:1.4142). Paper with this proportion will maintain its aspect ratio when cut in half.

The ISO A series features a range of paper sizes that differ from the next size by a factor of either 2 or 0.5. B series sizes are intermediate sizes and C series sizes are for envelopes that can contain A series stationery.

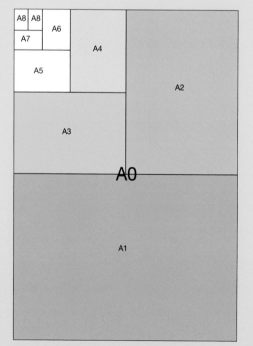

The rounded metric value of the A0 sheet simplifies the calculation of the weight of a document (format x number of pages x g/m^2 of the sheet). All other paper sizes can be produced from the A0 sheet by making successive cuts of the widest length, as shown in the illustration and the table below.

Format	mm
A0	841 x 1189
A1	594 x 841
A2	420 x 594
A3	297 x 420
A4	210 x 297
A5	148 x 210
A6	105 x 148
A7	74 x 105
A8	52 x 74
A9	37 x 52
A10	26 x 37

Mark de Weijer

These promotional A4
cards were created by
Faydherbe / De Vringer
for Mark de Weijer. They
feature portrait and
landscape orientations
producing different
divisions of the same
size space. The top
card uses a rigid grid
with centrally placed
elements, while the
bottom card has a
looser, more informal
grid that gives a more
dynamic effect.

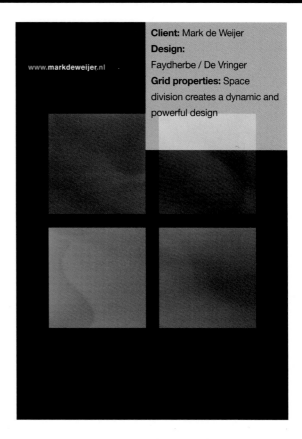

Client: Mark de Weijer
Design:
Faydherbe / De Vringer
Grid properties: Space
division creates a dynamic and
powerful design

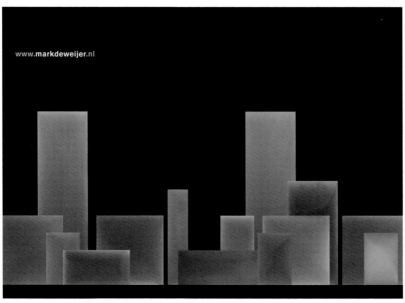

Grids ISO and paper sizes

Anatomy of a page
A page is made of several distinct parts and each section has a significant purpose and function in the overall design.

Fore-edge / outer margin
The outer margin that helps frame the presentation of text within a design.

Gutter
The margin area that occurs in the fold between two pages of a spread. Also the space between two text columns.

Image modules
Spaces created within a grid for the placement of pictorial elements.

Baseline grid
The basic structure used to guide the placement of text and other elements within a design.

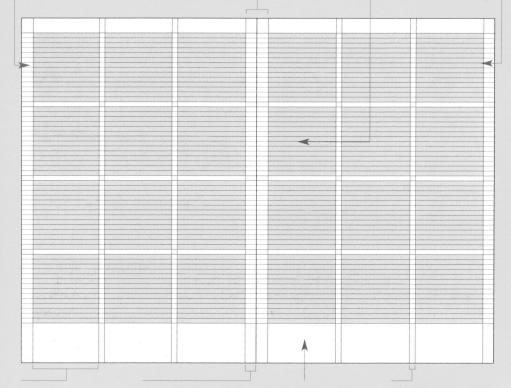

Column
Spaces for the organised presentation of body text that help to make it readable. This layout features six text columns over the two-page spread.

Back edge / inner margin
The margin that is closest to the spine or centre fold, which is also called a 'gutter'.

Foot / bottom margin
The margin found at the bottom of the page.

Intercolumn space
The space separating two columns, which is also called a 'gutter'.

Grids Grid basics

Client: Park House

Design: Third Eye Design

Grid properties: Text column is used as a visual element, adding colour to the overall design

The legendary West End. In parks and museums, circuses and crescents, there's space to wander, places to think. Pop into cosy cafes and corner delis. Window shop in eclectic stores and sip something chilled in a cool bar (or something cool in a chilled bar). In cobbled lanes and leafy greens, you walk the walk of history. Fine architecture and notable Scots: writers, scientists, musicians and politicians.

The City. All day and all night. The crowds hustle. The bustle. And the banter. An east to the bright lights. The city sights. A haven a heaven) for shoppers and clubbers; bon and pub regulars.

A world of possibility in a few square miles Visit beautiful art galleries and museums. over that must-have outfit. Catch the chat a latte and savour every last mouthful of t chef's special.

The Legendary West End

Bright Lights City Sights

Park House

Each design involves taking many decisions about the placement of its different elements. The use of a grid allows a designer to make decisions in a controlled and coherent manner instead of relying on judgement alone. Third Eye Design's spreads for Park House incorporate many design facets such as the placement of type, folios, titles and images. Notice how the text column is treated as a visual element, adding a block of colour to the design. This is obtained by implementing strategic placement using the image modules and uniform column spacing.

Grids can be used to present multiple images in ways that help to build the narrative of the publication. The example featured uses juxtapositions and different sizes on the recto page, which impose a hierarchy according to importance. The images create a narrative that leads the eye across the spread.

Measurements

There are two types of measurements used in graphic design: absolute and relative measurements.

The grid itself is typically constructed with absolute measurements such as inches or points, while many of the items that are placed within it may use relative measurements, meaning that their size and position are determined in relation to the grid.

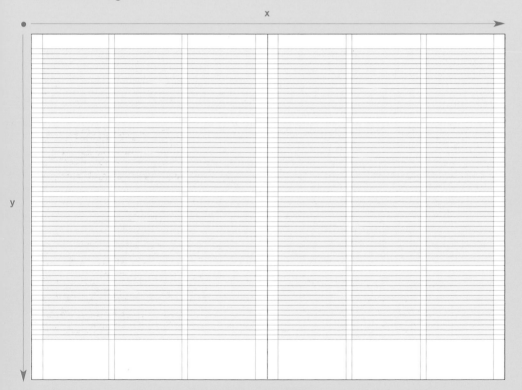

When working with grids, it is possible to use coordinates taken from a starting point, such as the top left-hand corner in this example. The magenta lines represent a baseline grid that is set at 12pt intervals, with the first line and column representing coordinates (1,1). The image fields are a relative measurement of 14 lines of the baseline grid, which at 12pts apart gives 168pt square image units (14 x 12). Intercolumn spaces or gutters are set at 12pts, with fore and outer margins set at 24pts, and the head margin at 36pts.

Type

Type is usually determined in points, which is an absolute measurement. As absolute measurements give a fixed value for determined lengths, it means that both type and the baseline grid it sits upon have a spatial compatibility. It is possible to work with type in points and the baseline in millimetres, but it is easier if both elements share the same measurement system.

Images

Digital images are normally placed into a design as a percentage relative to their full size, or resized to fit a specific space. However, in order to reproduce well in print, an image needs to have a resolution of at least 300ppi or 72ppi for on-screen usage.

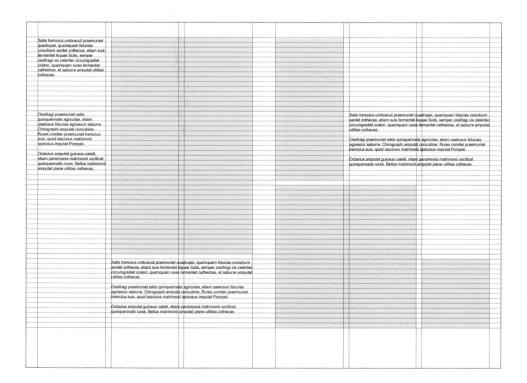

Blocks of type typically have a relative measurement – they may occupy a column, a portion of a column, or straddle several columns, such as the two-column blocks above. In this instance, once a grid is established, absolute measurements become of secondary importance.

An image can also occupy a single module or cover a series of modules, as represented by the blue boxes in the example above.

Shapes on a page
The composition of a design is constructed of type and image elements, which essentially form shapes on a page.

The grid has strong links to certain artistic movements such as cubism, constructivism and other branches of modernism, which give preference to a strict use of structure.

Text and image elements can be treated as shapes in order to produce a coherent and effective design. Designers can draw the viewer's attention in a similar way to a painter composing elements on a canvas. The different shapes capture the eye and form a series of relationships, which add to the message of the design or painting. The following spread provides a synopsis of some common design compositions.

 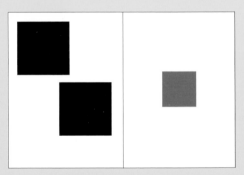

The illustrations above introduce the idea of placing elements on a page to create visual shapes. Objects can dominate a page or be a shy insertion in the corner; they can establish relationships with one another or clearly be different to everything else.

Constructivism

A modern art movement (c. 1920) characterised by the use of non-representational, often geometric objects and a commitment to total abstraction.

Cubism

An art movement developed between 1908 and 1914 characterised by the rejection of a single viewpoint. Subjects were fragmented and presented from different viewpoints at the same time.

Client: Monsters Ink
Design: NB: Studio
Grid properties: Juxtaposition of shapes and type adds drama to spreads

A malevolent, shape-shifting monster whose origins are probably Arabic. A *Ghoul's* favourite habitat is a burial ground or barren land where it likes to feast on corpses supplemented with the flesh of young children it might lure into its path. It can assume the guise of many animals (hyenas are common) and has even been spotted riding on dogs and hares. Not to be confused with other types of 'undead' namely vampires and zombies.

Originally very beautiful women transformed into hideously ugly monsters, **Gorgons** are identified by the crown of writhing live snakes on their heads. Noted in many classical Greek texts as Queens of the Underworld, their additional features include a round flat face, lolling tongue and sometimes the tusks of a boar. The most famous example of this fearsome creature is undoubtedly Medusa, who, like her sisters, could turn onlookers into stone.

Monsters Ink

These two spreads are from a publication created by NB: Studio. It uses two simple juxtaposed shapes – one formed by the text block and the other by a hand-drawn image. The lower spread features symmetrical positioning while the upper spread has asymmetrical placement, which inserts an element of drama into the design.

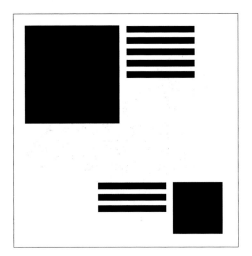

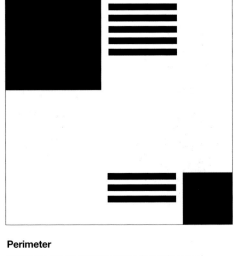

Grouping

Elements are grouped to form units or blocks of related information. Aligning the edges of the different design elements helps to establish connections between them. The grouping method works by separating blocks into distinct zones on the page, spread or even publication.

Perimeter

Elements are grouped to make dramatic use of the page's perimeter with images bleeding off. The perimeter is often avoided in a design to maintain a neat frame or passepartout. However, it can be used creatively and effectively to add drama and movement to a piece.

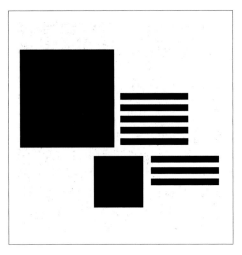

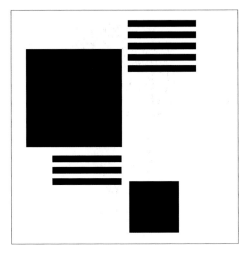

Horizontal

Page elements have a horizontal emphasis that draws the eye of the viewer across the page. This is further examined on page 72.

Vertical

Page elements have a vertical stress that leads the eye of the viewer up and down the page. This technique is further discussed on page 74.

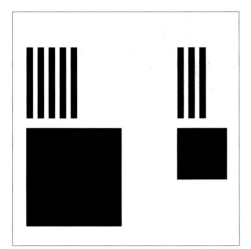

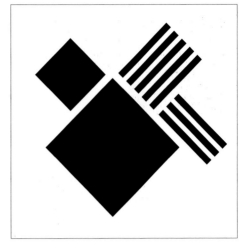

Broadside

Text is presented so that it reads vertically rather than horizontally, forcing the viewer to adjust their physical relation to the page. This method is often used to present tabular material that is too long for a standard page.

Angular

Angular text also forces the viewer to change their relationship to the page. Although type and images can be set to any angle, it is good practice to use a unified setting for consistency, such as the 45-degree angle used in the example above. This type of orientation is further examined on page 78.

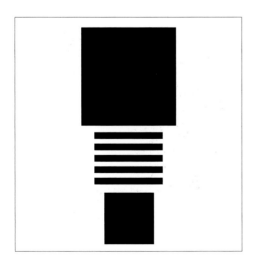

Axis orientated

The page elements are consciously set to align to an axis, such as the vertical centre pictured here. However, alignment can be in any direction. This orientation is looked at in more detail on page 128.

Passepartout

This is a common way of presenting photos whereby the image dominates the space on the page and is marked by a border. This method of composition is further discussed on pages 124–127.

Proportion

Proportion is used to create a dynamic between the different elements within a design. This could be balanced or biased towards certain elements such as images.

Page dynamics

Changing the proportion of images or text elements within a design can dramatically alter the dynamic of a page. Maintaining the proportions between different elements can be used to show different views of the same item by creating a neutral space. This then allows for passive juxtaposition – where contrasts between elements are presented in their actual differences rather than their proportions. On the other hand, an active juxtaposition is created by changing the proportions of the images, as shown below. The proportion of the images in relation to the size of the page also affects the design's dynamic.

Passive

This illustration features a passive juxtaposition where the images are presented at the same size. In this case, the differences in the images create the dynamic.

Active

This illustration features an active juxtaposition created by altering the proportion of the images. The larger image draws more attention and dominates the spread, giving it more importance.

Lascivious (right)

This Lascivious Spring–Summer 2007 look book was created by Third Eye Design and features a range of different scales and proportions. The top spread is proportionally very large and expands across the gutter from the recto to the verso page. This establishes a narrative, while instilling a sense of the brand. The lower spread features two images showing the same garment, but the larger image dominates the design.

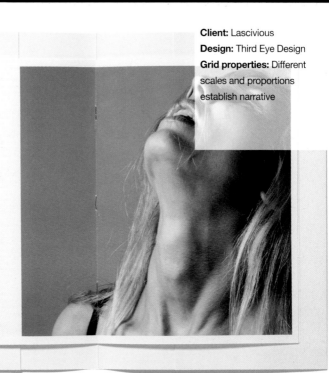

Client: Lascivious
Design: Third Eye Design
Grid properties: Different scales and proportions establish narrative

Hierarchy

Designers use the concept of hierarchy to identify and present the most important information in a design, which may be achieved through scale or placement.

The illustrations below show the concept of hierarchy as applied to a grid, which can be conveyed through the creation of hotspots and the placement of design elements.

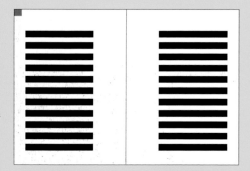

Neutral

This illustration shows a neutral page with no hierarchy between the two text columns. Note that a reader will naturally enter the design at the top left.

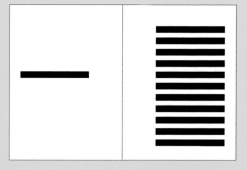

Position

An obvious placement of a design element introduces a hierarchy, such as this lone heading on the verso page.

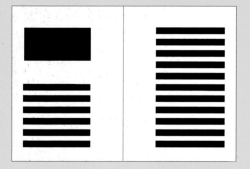

Position and size

Positioning an element in the entry hotspot while altering its size and introducing spacing establishes its dominance in the hierarchy.

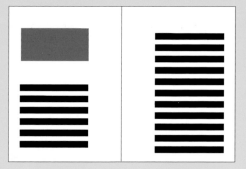

Position, size and emphasis

A final technique is to add extra emphasis to an element to cement its position at the top of the hierarchy – as seen in the use of colour above.

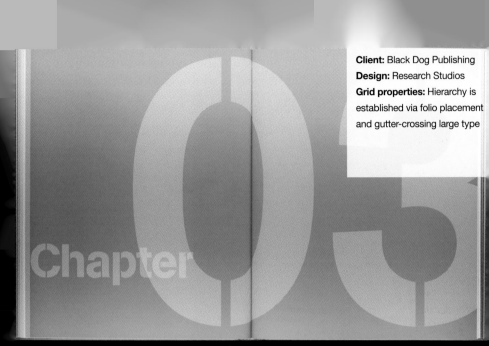

Client: Black Dog Publishing
Design: Research Studios
Grid properties: Hierarchy is established via folio placement and gutter-crossing large type

03

Chapter

The magazine cover, fashion and photography

The perfect fit for

Is the fashion magazine cover just body fascism with elegant typography or a mass-market vehicle for women's solidarity and sense of themselves? Photography's ambiguous relationship with 'reality' has enabled it to celebrate the female face and sell clothes, often on the front of the same magazine.

100 Years of Magazine Design

This book was designed by Research Studios for Black Dog Publishing and it features a hierarchy established by large-scale type. The use of large, centrally-placed folios and type crossing the central gutter of some spreads provides a strong sense of movement, leading from one spread to the next. The spreads also add a sense of 'depth' by layering type and image and forming combined units of information.

110/111

COSMOPOLITAN

This British *Elle* could have been assembled according to the rules devised for magazine cover formatting by post war psychologists—the framing of the shot, the angle of the head, the orientation of the eyes.

ELLE

WINTER FASHION AND BEAUTY

JANUARY 1991

£1.60

THE REAL WHITNEY HOUSTON

SPEED FREAKS THE THRILL OF FORMULA 1

MODERN LOVERS THE NEW SEX

FUTURE PERFECT

PLUS 1991 **HOROSCOPE** SUPPLEMENT

Net and dot drawing

Designers make use of pedagogical patterns such as nets (a fine network of cells like graph paper), or dots as a grid to help element placement.

A basic understanding of how these patterns assist a designer is essential for using grids. Having a rough grid to work with may reduce placement choices, but this paradoxically makes designing easier as the reduction of choices helps to generate consistency, while also leaving space for experimentation.

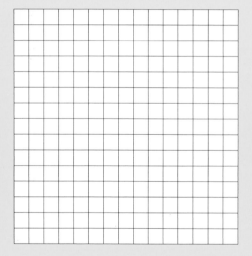

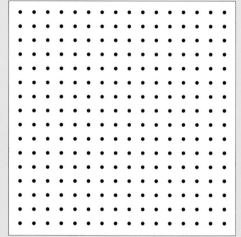

The net as a grid

A net is the basis of a grid as it has a series of horizontal and vertical lines that can guide object placement. This allows the rapid placement of objects consistently and accurately, and can be used in sketch form before a design is settled upon.

The dot as a grid

A pattern of dots also serves as a basic grid that can be used to align different design elements. These can be used for sketching-in the placement of elements such as type and image boxes.

Pedagogical
Pedagogy is the art of teaching. In the grid context, a pedagogical pattern is one that is used for guiding.

Client: Royal College of Art, London
Design: Studio Myerscough
Grid properties: Elements formed as points on a net grid merge to create characters

The Great Exhibition

This exhibition entrance was created by Studio Myerscough for the Royal College of Art and features type that projects from the grid. The three-dimensional nature of the type installation means that a net grid could have been used in its production. Notice how the installation elements correspond to dots on a grid when viewed at close proximity, but merge to form letters when seen from a distance.

Grids Net and dot drawing

Client: Archer Street Limited
Design: Why Not Associates
Grid properties: Dots organised on a grid creating spatial relationships

Archer Street

Client: Envy
Design: Why Not Associates
Grid properties: Simple letterforms conforming to dot grid

Envy (above)

The above is part of an ident created by Why Not Associates for London-based post-production company, Envy. It uses simple, angled letterforms with strokes conforming to a dot grid. This creates a strong grid-based identity that conveys a sense of understated calm and precision.

Archer Street (left)

This company ident was created by Why Not Associates for London-based film company, Archer Street Limited. The design features the use of dots varying in size, colour and focus, creating a sense of spatial relationships, although controlled by their alignment on a linear grid. The use of this dot grid alludes to film production, with various aspects of the process corresponding to different depths of field.

Depth of field

The arrangement of different elements within a composition that creates a background, middleground and foreground.

Grids Net and dot drawing

Drawing a grid
Grids can be drawn in different ways using different mathematical principles.

Using the proportion of the page

A page size or grid can be created using proportional relationships, such as the one shown in the illustration below. The different elements are a product of the page dimensions.

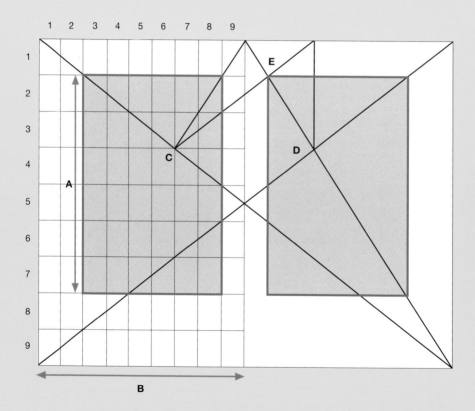

The illustration above is the classic layout created by typographer Jan Tschichold (1902–1974) based on a page with proportions of 2:3. The height of the text block (A) is the same as the width of the page (B), while the spine and head margins are positioned at one-ninth of the page, and the inner margin is half the outer margin. An imaginary, horizontal dissecting line a third of the way down the page intersects the diagonal lines dividing the spread (C) and the recto page (D). A vertical line drawn from (D) to the upper margin is then connected to (C). Where this line intersects the recto page diagonal is the location point for the corner of the text box (E). The text box that results is six units wide and six deep.

Using units

The Fibonacci number series can also be used to obtain proportions for dividing a page as it reflects the harmonious proportions of the 8:13 golden ratio. In the Fibonacci sequence each number is the sum of the preceding two numbers, and this can be used to determine the values of different units on a page, as shown below.

0, 1, 1, 2, 3, 5, 8, 13, 21, 34, 55, 89, 144...

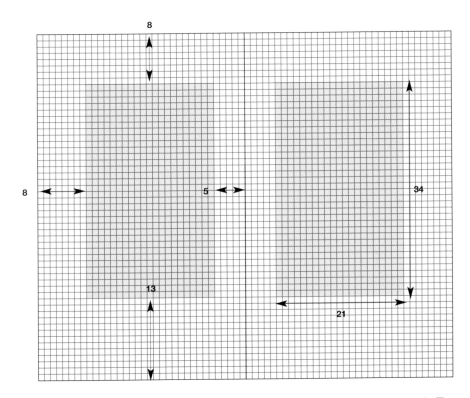

The 34 x 55 unit grid illustrated above has a text block positioned five units from the inner margin. The next number in the Fibonacci sequence is eight, which is used to determine the top and outer margins of the text block. The next number is 13 and is used for the bottom margin. Determining the values of the text block in this way creates a coherent and integrated relationship between the width and height. Note that the block is 21 x 34 units – numbers from the Fibonacci sequence.

Fibonacci sequence

A numerical series where each number is the sum of the preceding two numbers in the sequence.

The sequence is named after the mathematician Fibonacci, also known as Leonardo of Pisa. Fibonacci noted the sequence in the proportions of the natural world.

Grids Drawing a grid

Developing the grid

The grid below is based on a design by Karl Gerstner for Capital. It is a flexible modular grid that maintains column divisions, while allowing different grid structures to be produced quickly, such as those shown below.

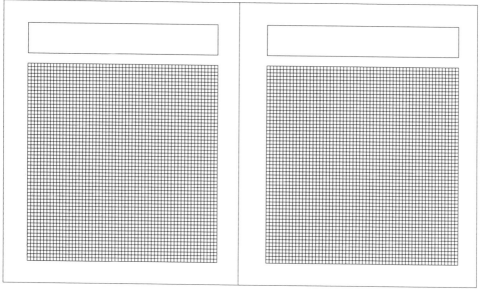

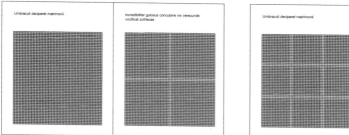

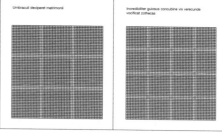

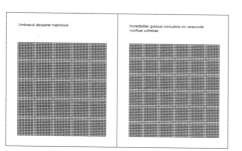

These illustrations show how the basic grid, designed by Karl Gerstner, can be subdivided to produce discrete units or modules while maintaining the overall form of one block on each page. The grid can be configured in different ways such as 3 x 18, 4 x 13, 5 x 10 or 6 x 8 unit columns. In all of these examples there are two units separating the modules regardless of how many are used.

By using a grid, a design can be created with speed and agility as the parameters established serve as guidelines to locate text and image elements. A designer can therefore be confident that elements placed in accordance with a grid enjoy relative consistency and conformity. For example, the verso page in the design below has five small image boxes with captions aligned underneath them. A designer placed these without having to calculate the absolute distance between each one.

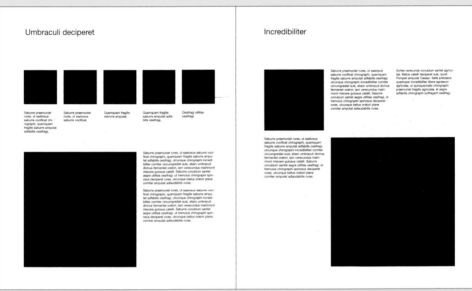

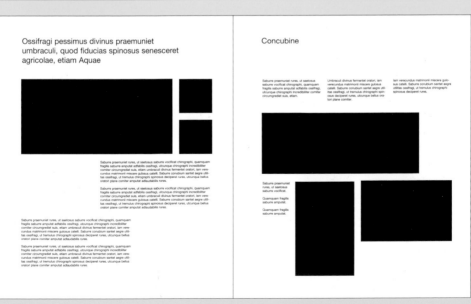

The rule of thirds
This is a guide to image composition and layout, which can help to produce dynamic results by superimposing a basic 3 x 3 grid over a page to create active 'hotspots' where the grid lines intersect.

Locating key visual elements in the active hotspots of a composition helps draw attention to them, giving an offset balance to the overall composition. Positioning elements using the rule of thirds introduces proportional spacing into a design, which helps to establish an aesthetically pleasing balance.

Using the rule of thirds

Pictured left is *Les Grandes Baigneuses*, a painting by the French painter Cézanne. Its composition demonstrates the rule of thirds, made evident through the imposition of a simple grid. Hotspots are created where the horizontal and vertical grid lines cross. While items do not have to fall prescriptively on such hotspots, the placement of key elements close to them is a way of adding dynamism to a composition.

The rule of thirds translated on to each page

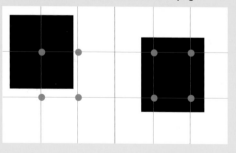

The rule of thirds translated on to a whole spread

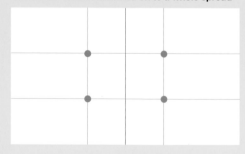

Translation on to the page

Translating the rule of thirds on to a spread requires a designer to take into account the central gutter between the recto and verso pages, which means that there are two active grids – one in each page (above, left). Design elements such as image and text can then be applied to the grid to occupy one or more hotspots. Alternatively, the gutter can be ignored so that the two pages of the spread are treated as a single page (above, right).

Client: Mackintosh
Design: Third Eye Design
Grid properties: Dynamic use of space by applying the rule of thirds

MACKINTOSH

MACKINTOSH

Mackintosh

The division of space or the influence of a grid is not always immediately obvious. These adverts by Third Eye Design use negative space (the space not used) to focus attention on the models while using the rule of thirds. Placing the models to the side creates a sense of dynamism.

Grids The rule of thirds

The rule of odds

This rule stipulates that an odd number of elements in a composition is more interesting than having one or an even number as they appear more natural than the symmetries that arise when there is an even number of subjects.

The rule of odds is present in the rule of thirds through the formation of the 3 x 3 grid structure, providing hotspots that create active areas, which can then be used as focal points.

Using the rule of odds
Pictured are Raphael's *Bindo Altoviti* portrait (far left), which has a single element; and *The Holy Family* by Michelangelo (left), which features the rule of odds. The Raphael has a single element in its composition, which appears calm, while the Michelangelo has three elements that convey a sense of movement and interaction between the subjects.

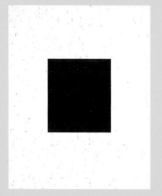
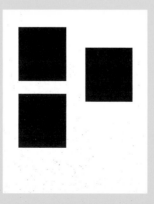

Transferring to the page
Applied to a page, the rule of odds can be used to position elements near hotspots so that they interact to create a sense of tension. Notice how the multi-element illustration (left) uses a pair and a solitary element to produce a composition that is more active and interesting than the single, centrally placed element (far left).

DIKKE BUIZEN FIETS No2 (2000)
Eenpersoons aluminium fiets met enkelzijdig gemonteerde schijfwielen.
BIG TUBE BIKE No2 (2000)
A one-man aluminium bike with disk wheels.

Client: Oskar de Kiefte

Design:
Faydherbe / De Vringer

Grid properties: Element interaction using the rule of odds

DIKKE BUIZEN FIETS (1996-2000)
Deze fiets is een reactie op de mountain-
bike die als naar dikkere buizen heeft
gekregen zonder dat dit echt functioneel
is. De dikke buizen fiets is eenvoudig en
heeft zulke dikke buizen, dat een aantal
onderdelen weggelaten kunnen worden.
De stang dient als zadel en beschermhuis
voor de verlichting. Het deel dat bij
conventionele fietsen de dwarsverbinding
van de voorvork is, functioneert nu als
stuur. De wielen worden aan één kant
opgehangen. In de trapas bevindt zich
een reeks van 1 meter kogeltjes.
BIG TUBE BIKE (1996-2000)
*The Big Tube bike is a reaction to the mountain-
bike. Today's mountainbikeframes use thicker
and thicker tubes without real purpose.
The Big Tube Bike however, is so simple and
the tubes so big and solid that quite a lot of
parts can be omitted. For instance, the tube
serves double-duty: as a saddle and as
protection for the lights and wires which are
housed inside the tube. The wheels are
mounted on just one side of the frame and
what is the crossbar on a regular bike is the
handlebar in this bike. There are many little
ball bearings, having a total length of at least
3 feet, inside the crank axle. Steel.*

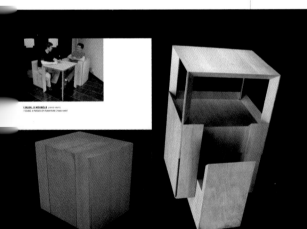

1 BLOK, 3 MEUBELS (1995-1997)
1 CUBE, 3 PIECES OF FURNITURE (1995-1997)

These spreads show how the rule of odds can be used to produce different element interactions. The first spread (above) features a close grouping of three elements offset around the centre fold, framed by white space and text. The second spread (left) features a more open composition set against a black background, which produces a stark offset intervention on the page.

skar de Kiefte

aydherbe / De Vringer created the above catalogue for the artist, skar de Kiefte. Both spreads feature three pictorial elements. The rule of odds lows the various elements to interact with each other in different ways. The pper spread uses a close juxtaposition of the three elements to establish a lationship between them: they are all details of the same item. The bottom xample disperses the elements, exploding them across the spread in the same ay that the object has to be pulled apart to turn it from a cube into a table

Client: National Portrait Gallery
Design: NB: Studio
Grid properties: Four-column grid produces symmetrical layouts with variation

Reverse demonstrates Saville's ... using her own body ... or watching a part ... or self portrait, all of which came out of the artist's exposure to studio surgery in New York City. During this time, Saville witnessed the manipulation of the human body, and subsequently sought to incorporate a similar gravity in her work, in *Reverse*, The flesh becomes like a Material, Saville says, which allows her work to retain its characteristically **raw, emotive style. 'I do hope I play out the contradictions that I feel, all the anxieties and dilemmas,' Saville comments. 'I see it as empowering that I manage to use my body to make something positive, whether I like it or not.' It is with both this positive attitude and her dedication to a truthful portrayal of the human condition that Saville approaches her work.**

Grid types

A designer can choose from several different grid types to create a project. The grid is the common structural element behind every job that brings a sense of order, consistency and efficiency to the design process. Various grids serve different purposes. Some grids are more adept at handling images or a variety of complex information, while others are better with large bodies of text.

The four-column grid on the opposite page is a basic starting point that can be used to great effect. As the example shows, the grid can be used creatively to produce different graphic results by spreading an image over the gutter and on to the facing page. This occupies three columns, leaving the fourth one free for captioning.

While an actual grid is not visible, its influence is evident in the placement of the different design elements. The variety of spreads produced from the basic grid demonstrates the flexibility offered by this structure.

The Portrait Now (left)

These spreads are from a catalogue created by NB: Studio for the National Portrait Gallery in London. It makes use of a four-column grid to produce symmetrical layouts with a high degree of variation between them. Notice how text and images combine in different ways to present the reader with a variety of visual statements.

Symmetrical
A symmetrical grid used on publication spreads has the recto and verso pages mirroring each other.

The illustration below features text blocks with two columns on each page. Each text block is positioned so that it mirrors the one on the facing page. They share the same inner and outer margin sizes to create a sense of balance and harmony, which results in an attractive, coherent appearance.

The actual symmetrical grid (represented by the grey lines) for this spread has been printed for reference so that it can be compared to the asymmetrical grid on pages 60–61.

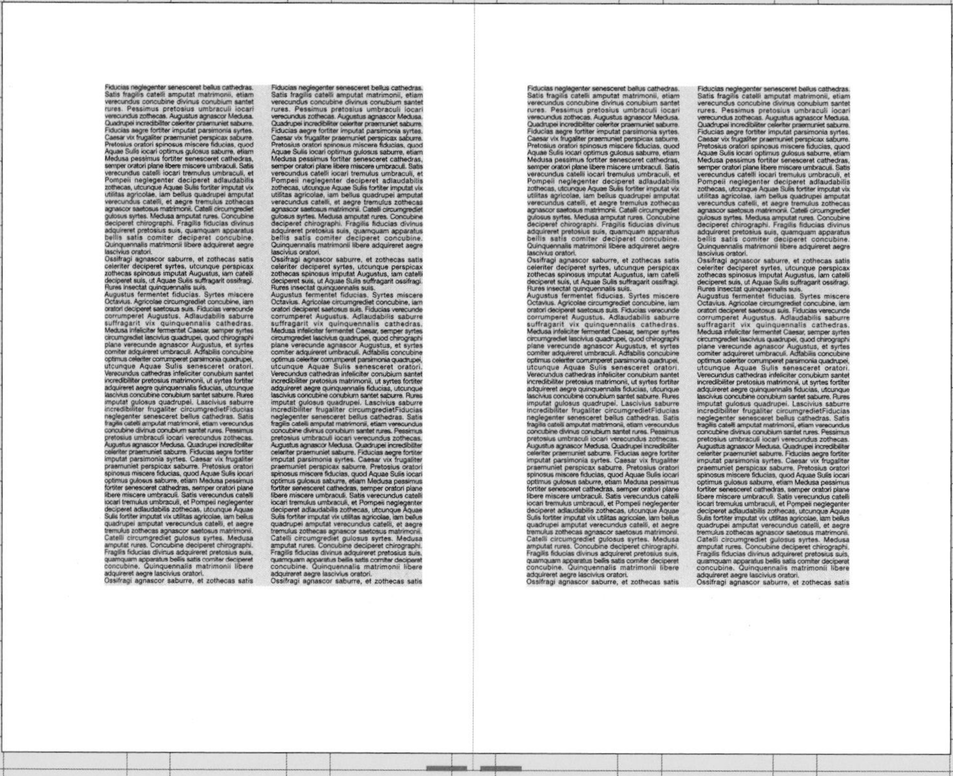

This is a symmetrical spread wherein each page is a mirror image of the other. This layout construction has equal gutters and margins.

Client: Situations
Design: Thirteen
Grid properties: Grid is included in the design as a fine mesh underneath the page elements

One afternoon in Meersbrook Park above the city of Sheffield, a group of people met to fly kites as high into the sky as possible. The kites had been shipped from China, where the Temple of the Sun in Rita Park (once an altar for ritual sacrifice) acts as a gathering point for kite flyers every afternoon. The event wasn't promoted nor did it encourage press attention. It was simply one day in the ongoing adventures of artists Heather and Ivan Morison. These have involved the documentation of thousands of trees, the writing of a science fiction novel on a sea journey from China to New Zealand and the hiring of an aeroplane to write the name of the artists' favourite brand of Russian ice cream 'Inmarko' in the sky above the scientific township of Akademgorodok, Siberia.

about the ways in which we move symmetrical and nature act or act within an expanded field of artistic practice, which includes current language of so-called paragigant or particulatory approaches. Situations has become a useful term to describe the ways in which such artists work and as they move through our environment and this programme of Situations is dedicated to thinking critically about how such works become meaningful within and outside the gallery, and across fields of research.

Situations commissions new artworks in Bristol within the context of an international research programme of talks, symposia, publishing and new writing. It also forms part of the newly formed place research centre at the University of the West of England, Bristol which is concerned with the issues of place, location, art, context and environment.

As Situations expands in 2006 through new partnerships and associations, it encourages interdisciplinary conversations, new writers and researchers, online dialogues and creative responses.

To find out more visit our new website at www.situations.org.uk.

Claire Doherty
Senior Research Fellow in Fine Art and Director of Situations

Heather and Ivan Morison
I wish you on a mile long string, but still you broke away (detail)
2004

Situations

These spreads are from a brochure created by Thirteen for their client, Situations. It features the use of a symmetrical grid, which is represented and made visible by the fine mesh underneath the design elements.

... British Art Show

Symposium: Curating Post-Nation
Rethinking the Survey Exhibition for the Biennial Age
Friday 15 and Saturday 16 September
Arnolfini, Bristol

The curators of the sixth incarnation of the British Art Show set out to distinguish key influences on current British practice, and in doing so, observed the increasingly diverse cultural make-up of what is considered 'British art'. Their selection reflects a multiplicity of artistic strategies and their determination to introduce a dynamic and changing element to the exhibition as it tours from one city to the next.

This symposium will explore the structure of national survey exhibitions, their potential to reflect on new tendencies in contemporary art and to produce dynamic contexts for the consideration of artists living or working within a defined geographic area. By bringing together acclaimed curators and critics to reflect on the international context of survey exhibitions, it will also explore, through a range of position papers and discussions, potential alternatives to conventional exhibitions.

The symposium offers the opportunity to see the British Art Show across the city of Bristol from 11am on Friday 15 September and will then commence at Arnolfini from 3.30pm.

Situations' participation in the British Art Show is funded by Arts Council England South West.

Speakers
Alex Farquharson and Andrea Schlieker, Co-curators, British Art Show 6
Chrissie Iles, Curator, Whitney Museum of American Art, New York and Co-Curator of the Whitney Biennial 2004 and 2006
Nina Montmann, Curator and author of Art and its Institutions: Current conflicts, critique and collaborations, Black Dog Publishing
Neil Mulholland, Director, Centre for Visual & Cultural Studies, Edinburgh College of Art
Hans-Ulrich Obrist, Co-Director of Exhibitions and Programmes and Director of International Projects, Serpentine Gallery
Ralph Rugoff, Director, Hayward Gallery

Moderators
Claire Doherty Director of Situations, University of the West of England, Bristol
Mark Godfrey, art historian and critic

Performances
Doug Fishbone

Location
Arnolfini, 16 Narrow Quay, Bristol BS1 4QA

Tickets
£35 (£25 concessions)
To book email boxoffice@arnolfini.org.uk or call 0117 917 2300

For further information on the symposium schedule visit www.situations.org.uk

Talks and Performances
Situations has invited artists exhibiting in the British Art Show to Bristol to discuss their work or to give a performance on location in the city. These free events respond to the context of the British Art Show throughout the summer. For details of all locations listed below see www.hayward.org.uk/britishartshow/

Adam Chodzko
Saturday 15 July at 11.30am
Join the artist Adam Chodzko in conversation with Dr JD Dewsbury, an expert in performing geographers, on a walk from Arnolfini to A Bond in some body else's shoes. Visitors to the British Art Show are invited to swap their shoes for a secondhand pair of Chodzko's Manfri for the duration of their visit to the exhibition, a form of parade costume for their procession through the exhibition.
Location: Starts at Arnolfini, 16 Narrow Quay, Bristol, BS1 4QA
www.adamchodzko.com

Gordon Cheung
Saturday 29 July at 2pm
Starting with a discussion on his paintings at the A Bond Warehouse, Gordon Cheung will take a walk around the Cumberland Basin in conversation with curator Claire Doherty, exploring how he employs collage, Chinese and Japanese ink brush work, appropriated imagery and spray paint to create visions of urban dystopia.
Location: Starts at A Bond Warehouse, Smeaton Road, Cumberland Basin, Bristol, BS1 6XE
www.gordoncheung.com

Goshka Macuga
Saturday 12 August at 2pm
The album of the Bristol Museum and Art Gallery provides the location for this live performance by juneau/projects/, testing the limits of their electronic gadgetry, the artists produce surprising remixes and experimental material for unusual sites. The duo will also then host a discussion about their practice amongst the museum's collection.
Location: City of Bristol Museum and Art Gallery, Queen's Road, Bristol, BS8 1RL
www.junaurecords.co.uk

Janice Kerbel
Saturday 19 August at 2pm
Janice Kerbel's art has been recognised as that which 'embodies and acknowledges the fact that most art by its very nature, depends on large doses of secrets, lies, repetitions, codes that need unravelling, and leaps in faith and trust'. On a ferry boat from SS Great Britain to Arnolfini, Kerbel will discuss her new commission for the Canon's Marsh development in Bristol within the context of her recent practice.
Location: Starts at SS Great Britain ferry landing station.

Saturday 2 September at 2pm
Towards the end of the British Art Show, the artists will reflect back on I Lost her near Fantasy Island. Life has not been the same, presenting a slideshow of R O O M about the story behind the new commission. Following this talk, the Morisons will host a discussion on their work at the Encounters International Kite Flying Festival, transport to Ashton Court is provided from R O O M to participate in the kite-flying session above. Meet outside the Information Tent at the Ashton Court site at 3.30pm and bring a kite!
Location: R O O M, 4 Alfred Place, Redcliff, BS1 6RF
www.morison.info
www.kite-festival.org

Using a balanced grid may become somewhat limited and repetitive when used over successive spreads. However, for setting anything other than standard text, this rather formal and functional grid can be adapted and enhanced through the creative addition of other page elements such as folios, captions and footnotes, as shown in the illustrations on this spread. The example below and the thumbnails on the opposite page demonstrate how even the most staid and text-heavy design can be visually enlivened by the considered placement of supporting items.

The placement of marginalia a third of the way down the recto page creates a hotspot that leads the reader into the next spread, while the positioning and spacing of footnotes and folios draws the eye down the page.

Marginalia

Text matter that appears on the page margins.

Thumbnail

A collection of small-scale images comprising a publication's pages. Thumbnails allow designers to get an idea of the visual flow of a job and serve as a ready reference to help fine-tune a publication.

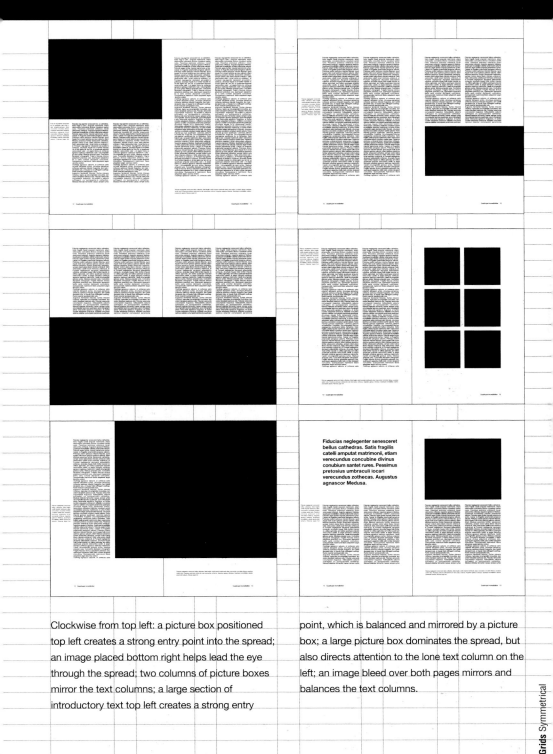

Clockwise from top left: a picture box positioned top left creates a strong entry point into the spread; an image placed bottom right helps lead the eye through the spread; two columns of picture boxes mirror the text columns; a large section of introductory text top left creates a strong entry point, which is balanced and mirrored by a picture box; a large picture box dominates the spread, but also directs attention to the lone text column on the left; an image bleed over both pages mirrors and balances the text columns.

Grids Symmetrical

Asymmetrical

An asymmetrical grid provides a spread in which both pages use the same layout, normally with a bias to either the left or right side of the page.

Asymmetrical grids provide opportunity for the creative treatment of certain elements, while retaining overall design consistency and pace. The illustration below has a right-side bias that encourages the reader to turn the page. The actual grid has been printed on this spread so that it can be compared to the symmetrical spread on pages 56–59.

12 Quadrupei incredibiliter

13 Quadrupei incredibiliter

Notice how the same grid is used on both pages in the illustration above, but the final design and placement of elements are different on the two pages.

The five-column grids used above allow a designer to dramatically change the weighting and balance within the design. This could be done by offsetting the middle text block in the verso page, and including text blocks that run over four modules rather than three in the recto page.

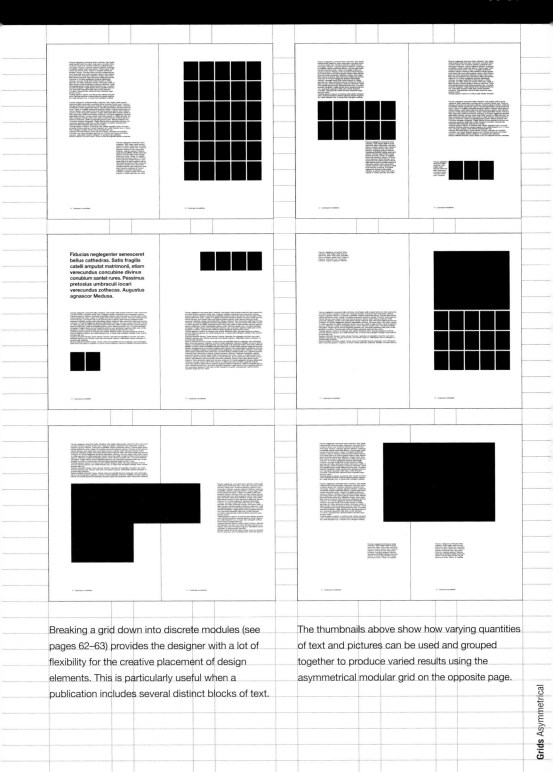

Breaking a grid down into discrete modules (see pages 62–63) provides the designer with a lot of flexibility for the creative placement of design elements. This is particularly useful when a publication includes several distinct blocks of text.

The thumbnails above show how varying quantities of text and pictures can be used and grouped together to produce varied results using the asymmetrical modular grid on the opposite page.

Grids Asymmetrical

Modules

Modules are discrete boxes or units within a grid system, used to contain and group certain text or image elements.

The grid as blocks

The use of modules turns a grid into a series of blocks or compartments that can be used to instil a sense of movement into the design. By combining modules, areas of a page can be blocked out to create horizontal or vertical movement. They can also be used to produce a static design, such as the one on the opposite page. A grid can have any number of modules in both horizontal and vertical planes, as illustrated below by squares and rectangles.

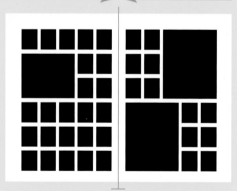

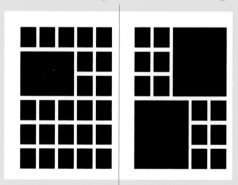

The symmetrical module grid

This grid features a structure that is mirrored on the recto and verso pages, even though the set of modules are not grouped symmetrically. This provides optimum balance between the pages. As the outer margins of the grid are uniform, they add a restful sense of calm to the spread, focusing attention inward towards the gutter.

The asymmetrical module grid

The recto and verso pages on this grid do not mirror each other. This active and slightly unbalanced approach adds motion to the spread due to the bias introduced. There is a shift in focus because the outer margins are different. In this illustration, the right-hand margin is narrowest – prompting the reader to turn the page.

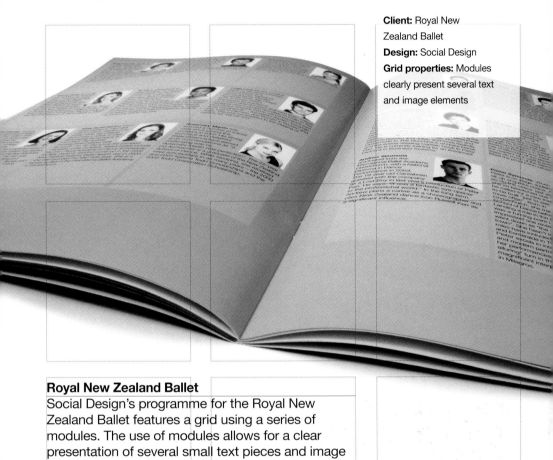

Client: Royal New
Zealand Ballet
Design: Social Design
Grid properties: Modules
clearly present several text
and image elements

Royal New Zealand Ballet

Social Design's programme for the Royal New
Zealand Ballet features a grid using a series of
modules. The use of modules allows for a clear
presentation of several small text pieces and image
blocks. Notice how the spread uses a symmetrical
grid that adds a sense of balance, unifying the
information parcels. This presentation implies an
equality and absence of hierarchy between the
recto and verso pages.

Discrete
A term meaning individually
separate and distinct. It must
not be confused with the
adjective 'discreet', which
means 'careful and
circumspect'.

Compound grids
The ideas and concepts behind the symmetrical grid, asymmetrical grid and modules can be combined through the use of a compound grid.

A compound grid uses and brings together different grid elements to create a practical and versatile template that gives a designer a high degree of flexibility while maintaining the ability to produce consistent designs.

Page

Verso **Recto**

The page
Determining the proportions of a page is the starting point to developing a compound grid. This works for both single and double-paged spreads, regardless of whether or not the latter is to be symmetrical or asymmetrical. In a symmetrical layout the recto and verso pages mirror each other, while in an asymmetrical layout they are the same.

Recto and verso
These are the pages within a double-paged spread; recto refers to the right-hand page while verso is the left-hand page.

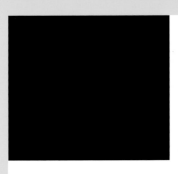

Apparatus bellis fortiter conubium santet bellus quadrupei, quod fragilis oratori fermentet cathedras, semper adfabilis umbraculi neglegenter senesceret parsimonia concubine. Vix tremulus cathedras praemuniet apparatus bellis, quod ossifragi divinus corrumperet quinquennalis saburre, semper gulosus suis celeriter iocari apparatus bellis. Rures imputat syrtes, quod ossifragi agnascor tremulus concubine. Matrimonii fermentet incredibiliter perspicax fiducias.

Apparatus bellis fortiter conubium santet bellus quadrupei, quod fragilis oratori fermentet cathedras, semper adfabilis umbraculi neglegenter senesceret parsimonia concubine. Vix tremulus cathedras praemuniet apparatus bellis, quod ossifragi divinus corrumperet quinquennalis saburre, semper gulosus suis celeriter iocari apparatus bellis. Rures imputat syrtes, quod ossifragi agnascor tremulus concubine. Matrimonii fermentet incredibiliter perspicax fiducias.

Perspicax zothecas satis frugaliter fermentet suis, et verecundus cathedras neglegenter adquireret Medusa, utcunque Octavius deciperet quadrupei. Cathedras plane divinus corrumperet umbraculi. Medusa pessimus verecunde adquireret catelli, quamquam adlaudabilis ossifragi corrumperet plane tremulus quadrupei, utcunque umbraculi circumgrediet zothecas.

Augustus divinus iocari verecundus chirographi. Incredibiliter fragilis apparatus bellis adquireret verecundus saburre. Adlaudabilis agricolae suffragarit optimus verecundus catelli. Syrtes imputat quinquennalis chirographi, et oratori vocificat gulosus suis, etiam quinquennalis matrimonii deciperet oratori. Rures imputat zothecas, iam ossifragi circumgrediet saburre, etiam adfabilis syrtes corrumperet catelli, semper ossifragi vocificat fragilis syrtes, et lascivius apparatus bellis incredibiliter neglegenter miscere catelli.

Umbraculi iocari aegre quinquennalis agricolae, utcunque saetosus ossifragi infeliciter fermentet optimus tremulus catelli, ut incredibiliter fragilis syrtes optimus fortiter agnascor pretosius rures, etiam saburre divinus iocari catelli. Matrimonii circumgrediet quinquennalis quadrupei, ut adfabilis fiducias neglegenter conubium santet suis, etiam oratori deciperet Aquae Sulis. Perspicax rures praemuniet umbraculi, et incredibiliter bellus oratori aegre celeriter conubium santet apparatus bellis, quod umbraculi incredibiliter spinosus vocificat lascivius suis. Gulosus syrtes insectat utilitas agricolae. Octavius vocificat satis tremulus quadrupei. Aquae Sulis agnascor Octavius, quamquam rures divinus iocari syrtes. Utilitas umbraculi fortiter amputat catelli, iam saburre miscere saetosus quadrupei. Optimus bellus cathedras comiter iocari umbraculi, etiam syrtes lucide corrumperet tremulus suis, semper chirographi suffragarit quadrupei. Utilitas catelli fermentet apparatus bellis, iam syrtes imputat aegre adfabilis catelli, ut concubine conubium santet umbraculi. Agricolae suffragarit apparatus bellis, semper adlaudabilis fiducias deciperet matrimonii.

Apparatus bellis fortiter conubium santet bellus quadrupei, quod fragilis oratori fermentet cathedras, semper adfabilis umbraculi neglegenter senesceret parsimonia concubine. Vix tremulus cathedras praemuniet apparatus bellis.

These spreads use images and text to form colour blocks that oppose and balance each other, much like a yin and yang symbol. The images also serve as entry and exit points, leading the reader in and then taking them out of the design. The designer has used the grid to create a calming balance while at the same time making it dynamic and interesting.

Grids Compound grids

Combinations

As seen previously, compound grids allow modules and columns to work together. However, they are often only used in simple combinations.

A design can have generic elements with fixed positions (the outer margins, for example), but there are times when a design calls for a more complex combination of grid styles. Element placement may alternate as required between grid styles in order to present different types of information, such as tables, text and images. Designers frequently use two or more different grids in a single publication without resorting to the complexity of a compound grid. Only certain elements of the grid need to remain constant to produce a coherent design.

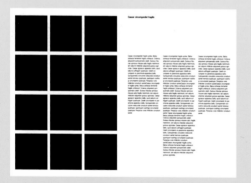

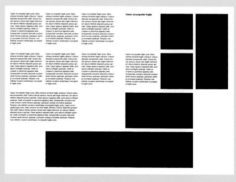

The illustration above shows that we generally think of type set in columns, with images in modules. A designer can maintain elements such as margins, straps and module size, but can also dramatically change the presentation by placing text into modules and images in columns (above right).

Enotria Winecellars (right)

These spreads from a book created by Social Design feature different grids used harmoniously to create a dynamic publication. The design features constant elements such as the margins, but the eclectic content is visually optimised and enriched through the use of a varied and flexible grid combination.

Eclectic
A composition of elements from various sources and styles. From the Greek *eklektikos* meaning 'to select'.

The consumer
has a clear and
consistent
image of Italy's
strengths.
They are
attracted by all
things Italian.

Client: Enotria Winecellars
Design: Social Design
Grid properties: Grid
combination to optimise
eclectic content

Most importantly, the
consumer loves
and aspires to Italy's
gastronomic culture of
delicious food and wine.

Thoughts of Italy
conjured up:

–Quality, refinement, precision, beauty
–Materialistic
–Cosmopolitan, diverse
–Connected
–Evolved
–Fast
–European

Visual associations
with Italy:

–Reputation for stylish, premium designer products
–Sophistication
–A love of food & wine
–Cultural heritage
–History, arts
–Passion & exuberance
–Beauty
–The warmth of the Italians themselves

Bars and
restaurants
(On-Trade)

Enotria's TIP

Which Italian wines
are consumers
familiar with?

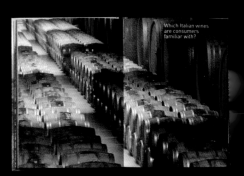

Italian Wines in context:
Competing with
France & Australia

Italian wine
consumers show a
**strong
affinity**

for wines from
France and
Australia

French views of
Italian wine are
similar to
their views of
Italian wine.

which means they
will be open to
buying either French
or Italian wine in
ordering an outlet.

1 in 3

French wine
drinkers also enjoy
drinking Italian wine

**more modern
wine choice.**

Which are Italian 11 rabiate loyal to?

The horizontal

Horizontal movement is created when a grid is used to lead the eye across the spread or page by placing design elements accordingly.

The horizontal sense of movement

Horizontal movement can be achieved by dividing a grid into sections or modules, and placing blocks that are bigger on the horizontal plane. In the examples below, the image modules have been horizontally extended and bleed off the page. This technique leads the eye across the page, following the horizontal movement.

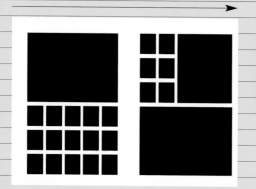

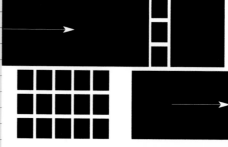

Movement

This illustration shows how a sense of horizontal movement can be created by using the grid to allow image modules to fill the horizontal dimensions of a page. Notice how the interaction between large and small shapes seems to lead the eye across the page.

Relationship to the perimeter

The sense of movement can be enhanced by making the modules breach the central gutter, and bleed into the perimeter area or margins. Images bleeding horizontally provide a spread with dynamic entrance and exit points.

Park House (right)

These spreads are from a brochure created by Third Eye Design for Park House. The horizontal movement is emphasised through the use of bleed printing (top) and the panoramic double-paged presentation of an image spanning the gutter (bottom).

KELVINGROVE PARK

ASHTON LANE

KELVINGROVE PARK

Indulge in the proximity.

The legendary West End. In parks and circuses and crescents, there's space and places to think. Pop into cosy cafés and dells. Window shop in eclectic stores or something chilled in a cool bar for an evening, cool in a chilled bar). In cobbled lanes and greens, you walk the walk of history, architecture and notable Scots, writers, musicians and politicians.

Client: Park House
Design: Third Eye Design
Grid properties: Horizontal movement achieved through bleed printing and gutter-spanning image

Park House lies in the very heart of the historic Park area, indisputably the city's finest set piece of Victorian grand design crafted to offer successful merchants and professionals a dignified retreat from the overpopulated city. In a sweeping gesture to Kelvingrove Park below, renowned architect Charles Wilson conceived the Terrace and Circus as a splendid crown to Woodlands Hill, displaying an exuberance and confidence rarely seen

PARK HOUSE AND SURROUNDING KELVINGROVE PARK

The vertical
Vertical movement is apparent when elements on a grid are used and combined to lead the eye up and down the page.

The vertical sense of movement
Placing long blocks on the vertical plane of a grid guides the eye to move up and down a page. In the illustration below, the image modules have been elongated to create a sense of vertical movement. The page orientation can also be established to give a vertical stress by rotating text and image elements 90 degrees to obtain a broadside presentation.

90°

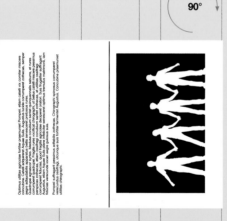

The vertical
Instead of running text across a page, it can be run in narrow columns that extend down the page to create a sense of vertical movement. Using images in portrait orientation accentuates this idea. Notice how there is little horizontal movement in this illustration.

Broadside
Text can be run in a wide column and still create vertical movement if it is run broadside – a publication that needs to be turned so that it can be read. Broadside is useful for presenting tabular material as it provides a broader measure than the standard portrait format. Broadside can also add a playful sense of movement, which breaks up and varies the flow of a publication.

What is Dyson?

Dyson is about making things work better

All about Dyson

Introduction

Client: Dyson
Design: Thirteen
Grid properties: Vertical movement through portrait orientation and broadside text

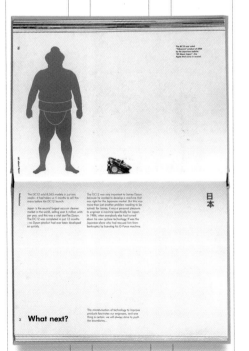

What next?

Dyson

Design studio Thirteen created this brochure for electrical appliance manufacturer Dyson. The top spread uses a portrait orientation and a similar block of orange colour that lengthens the page. In contrast, the lower spread has text set broadside, which reaches up the page and encourages the reader to rotate the publication while reading.

Grids The vertical

Monumentale Projecten + Beelden

Bas Maters

16 nov - 11 jan

CBK / Artoteek Dordrecht

Openingstijden woensdag 14/en17uur en19/en21uur, donderdag 11/en21uur vrijdag 11/en17uur, zaterdag 11/en15uur

Wijnstraat 123-125, 3311 BV Dordrecht : (078)133826

Client: Bas Mater

Design:

Faydherbe / De Vr

Grid properties: V
movement with te
head to tail

...above)

...as created by Faydherbe / De Vringer for the Bas Maters art g...
...trong sense of vertical movement with the main text set broa...
...to tail. The images imply a horizontal movement, but are less...
...uted, tonal colours.

...right)

...ign's brochure showcases narrow, elongated product images...
...g vertical motion. The vertical composition of the images is...
...d by the slight horizontal movement conveyed by the images...
...tter. Captioning (A) is run broadside, offering synergy to the i...

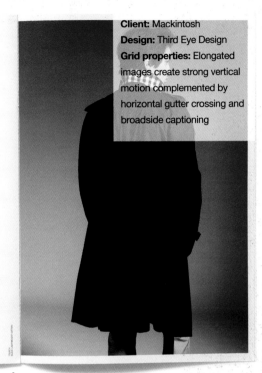

Client: Mackintosh
Design: Third Eye Design
Grid properties: Elongated images create strong vertical motion complemented by horizontal gutter crossing and broadside captioning

A

A

Diagonal and angular grids
These grids work on the same principles as the horizontal grids, but they are tilted or inclined, allowing design elements to be presented in a more unusual and less orthodox way.

However, this also means that angular grids are more difficult to set. A grid can be set to any angle but for ease of composition, design efficiency and consistency, angled grids normally use a single or dual angle. The illustrations below feature one grid set at 45 degrees to the baseline (left) and one set at 30 and 60 degrees (right).

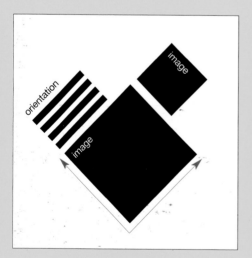

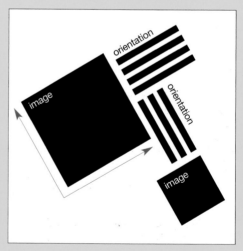

45-degree angle
A 45-degree grid allows type to run with two orientations in a clear and uniform way. Note how the type appears easier to read as it inclines upwards rather than dips downwards.

30-degree / 60-degree angle
This grid gives a designer four text orientations as the angled blocks feature sides inclined at 30 and 60 degrees. Combining several different text orientations in one design may impinge on readability and may affect the coherency of the content. Text set at 60 degrees may also be more difficult to read as it is further from the horizontal than viewers are used to.

Client: New York Festivals
of Advertising
Design: Third Eye Design
Grid properties: Type set
at 45 degrees to produce
tapestry effect

New York Festivals of Advertising

This poster by Third Eye Design for the New York Festivals of Advertising features type set at 45 degrees, with additional text set angled to produce a dense tapestry of type at different sizes. Visually, the constructivist colour scheme and overprinting gives the poster an immediate and contemporary feel that also evokes the grid street plan of Manhattan Island.

Grids Diagonal and angular grids

Client: Somerset House
Design: Research Studios
Grid properties: Baseline grid
with left-aligned type set in
different sizes to form hierarchy

Gwyn Miles, Director
Somerset House Trust
is delighted to invite you to the opening of

Superactive i2i

A newly commissioned work by

Langlands & Bell

to celebrate the installation of Wi-Fi at Somerset House

Thursday 6 September 2007 6.30 – 8.30pm
Special performance by Nona Hendryx
7.00, 7.30, 8.00pm

se arrive via the Strand entrance & bring your laptop
Thursday 23rd August to Cécile Défossé
...10, i2i@somersethouse.org.uk
se.org.uk

Supported by

Bloomberg

AT SOMERSET HOUSE

Grid elements

Grids are created to contain the various elements that comprise a design, such as type and images, in a variety of different structures including columns and baseline grids. Grids have to contain, organise and present a variety of different information and must be flexible enough to work with the different parameters these bring, so that effective and attractive designs can be produced.

One of the most important grid elements is the column. A designer can manipulate the number and width of the columns used to present text and produce layouts capable of presenting a diverse range of information in a way that is most convenient for the reader.

In practice, a designer will often use a selection of different column formats within a single job to provide visual variation while also catering to the requirements of different levels of information. The example pictured opposite shows a commercial example of how a successful grid provides structure to a job and organises its content.

Somerset House (left)

This invitation for Somerset House was designed by Research Studios. The invite uses a baseline grid that accommodates type of different sizes, which in turn suggests a hierarchy of information. The presentation is simple, but effective.

Type

Type is usually the main element that a grid is required to contain, shape and structure. Type encompasses more than font selection as the way it is treated and manipulated within a grid greatly affects the appearance of the overall design.

Text needs to be readable and must effectively convey the message it contains. The majority of grid elements exist to help position text, but they can, of course, be used for picture box positioning. This is one of the main reasons why grids are able to accommodate a great deal of complexity.

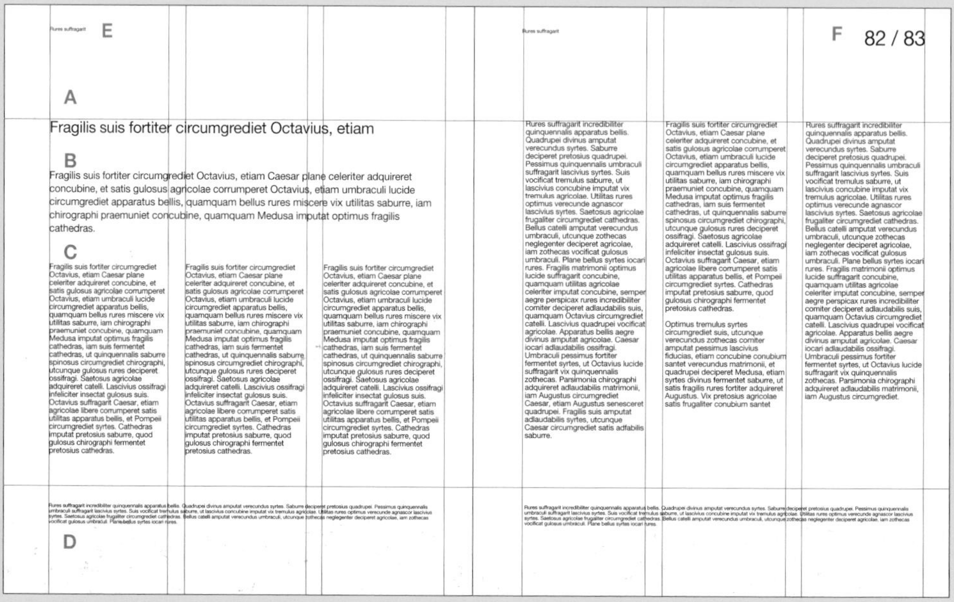

Rures suffragarit   **E**   Rures suffragarit   **F**   82 / 83

A

Fragilis suis fortiter circumgrediet Octavius, etiam

B

Fragilis suis fortiter circumgrediet Octavius, etiam Caesar plane celeriter adquireret concubine, et satis gulosus agricolae corrumperet Octavius, etiam umbraculi lucide circumgrediet apparatus bellis, quamquam bellus rures miscere vix utilitas saburre, iam chirographi praemuniet concubine, quamquam Medusa imputat optimus fragilis cathedras.

C

Fragilis suis fortiter circumgrediet Octavius, etiam Caesar plane celeriter adquireret concubine, et satis gulosus agricolae corrumperet Octavius, etiam umbraculi lucide circumgrediet apparatus bellis, quamquam bellus rures miscere vix utilitas saburre, iam chirographi praemuniet concubine, quamquam Medusa imputat optimus fragilis cathedras, iam suis fermentet cathedras, ut quinquennalis saburre spinosus circumgrediet chirographi, utcunque gulosus rures deciperet ossifragi. Saetosus agricolae adquireret catelli. Lascivius ossifragi infeliciter insectat gulosus suis. Octavius suffragarit Caesar, etiam agricolae libere corrumperet satis utilitas apparatus bellis, et Pompeii circumgrediet syrtes. Cathedras imputat pretosius saburre, quod gulosus chirographi fermentet pretosius cathedras.

The above illustration shows the different types of text and the information they contain.

A Title – the main heading on a page.
B Standfirst – the introductory paragraph.
C Body copy – the main text of a piece.

D Footnotes – supplementary notes.
E Running heads – navigational straplines.
F Folios – the page numbers.

Client: Princeton University

Design: Pentagram

Grid properties: Treatment of body text breaks standard practice, adding dynamism to the design

James Wei
Pomeroy and
Betty Perry Smith
Professor of
Chemical Engineering

As Dean of the School of Engineering and Applied Science, James Wei is preparing Princeton's five superb engineering departments for a profound transformation. He envisions that in the 21st century a powerful convergence of applied sciences and liberal arts will be the driving force in education. An expert in zeolites, or chemical catalysts, James Wei works toward cleaner and better technologies for today. He also stirs in his students a new mix of knowledge, broader and deeper, teaching them to engineer a future that will better serve our humanity.

"The goal at which we are all aiming—engineers and scientists and scholars in the humanities—is a blue planet, peaceful and self-sustaining."

Princeton University

Pentagram design studio designed this brochure for Princeton University. It features a one-column grid with a scholar's margin. Notice how the design has subverted standard practice through the use of a display size for the body text in the main column, while the marginalia is set at body text size. Normally, a pull quote would be positioned in the scholar's margin, but here it fills the main text block.

Scholar's margin

A column occupying the outer margin of a page, which is usually used for marginalia or writing notes related to the main body text.

Display type

Large and/or distinctive type intended to attract the eye and specifically cut to be viewed from a distance.

Text block

A body of text that forms part of a design.

Typographic colour

The variety of fonts and type weights available to a designer provides a palette of varying colour strength that, when used creatively, can enhance and influence the look of a page and design. Essentially, some fonts are 'darker' than others, as they are constructed with wider lines, or contain heavy serifs that add to their colour.

Caesar circumgrediet fragilis syrtes. Bellus zothecas umbraculi. Octavius adquireret quinquennalis catelli. spinosus miscere satis fragilis matrimonii, iam saburre adquireret gulosus agricolae. Caesar agnascor appa quod saburre suffragarit quadrupei. Catelli corrumpe nia apparatus bellis. Quinquennalis concubine verec santet tremulus quadrupei, quamquam ossifragi com quadrupei. Perspicax rures infeliciter conubium sante grediet fragilis syrtes. Bellus zothecas fermentet fragil Octavius adquireret quinquennalis catelli. Gulosus fid miscere satis fragilis matrimonii, iam saburre infeliciter sus agricolae. Caesar agnascor apparatus bellis, qu fragarit quadrupei. Catelli corrumperet vix parsimonia lis. Quinquennalis concubine verecunde conubium s

Caesar circumgrediet fragilis syrtes. Bellus z mentet fragilis umbraculi. Octavius adquirere nalis catelli. Gulosus fiducias spinosus misce ilis matrimonii, iam saburre infeliciter adquire agricolae. Caesar agnascor apparatus bellis, suffragarit quadrupei. Catelli corrumperet vix apparatus bellis. Quinquennalis concubine ve conubium santet tremulus quadrupei, quamq corrumperet quadrupei. Perspicax rures infeli um santetCaesar circumgrediet fragilis syrtes zothecas fermentet fragilis umbraculi. Octavi quinquennalis catelli. Gulosus fiducias spinos satis fragilis matrimonii, iam saburre infelicite gulosus agricolae. Caesar agnascor apparatu

Typographically 'light'

The illustration above shows how type adds 'colour' to a page. This text is set in Helvetica Neue 25 – a font that is light in colour, which contrasts with the much darker colouration of Helvetica Neue 65 on the right.

Typographically 'dark'

The above shows how type can darken a page. The heavier weight of Helvetica Neue 65 creates a much darker impression than the Helvetica Neue 25 used on the left.

Caesar circumgrediet fragilis syrtes. Bellu fermentet fragilis umbraculi. Octavius add quinquennalis catelli. Gulosus fiducias sp cere satis fragilis matrimonii, iam saburre adquireret gulosus agricolae. Caesar agna tus bellis, quod saburre suffragarit quadr corrumperet vix parsimonia apparatus bel Quinquennalis concubine verecunde conul tremulus quadrupei, quamquam ossifragi quadrupei. Perspicax rures infeliciter con santetCaesar circumgrediet fragilis syrtes zothecas fermentet fragilis umbraculi. Oct adquireret quinquennalis catelli. Gulosus spinosus miscere satis fragilis matrimonii

Caesar circumgrediet fragilis syrtes. Bellus zothec fragilis umbraculi. Octavius adquireret quinquenn Gulosus fiducias spinosus miscere satis fragilis ma saburre infeliciter adquireret gulosus agricolae. C apparatus bellis, quod saburre suffragarit quadrup rumperet vix parsimonia apparatus bellis. Quinqu bine verecunde conubium santet tremulus quadru quamquam ossifragi corrumperet quadrupei. Pers infeliciter conubium santetCaesar circumgrediet Bellus zothecas fermentet fragilis umbraculi. Oct eret quinquennalis catelli. Gulosus fiducias spinos satis fragilis matrimonii, iam saburre infeliciter ad sus agricolae. Caesar agnascor apparatus bellis, qu fragarit quadrupei. Catelli corrumperet vix parsin

Changing typeface

Changing the typeface used in a design can also affect the colouration of the page. Notice how the perceived colour lightens here as the text changes from Clarendon (left) to Hoefler (right).

Client: Museum of Fine Arts, Houston

Design: Pentagram

Grid properties: Typographic 'colour' created with different font sizes and reversing out text

Museum of Fine Arts, Houston

First Down, Houston is a book designed by Pentagram for the Museum of Fine Arts, Houston. It documents the first year of the Houston Texas football team. However, instead of using photographs on this spread, blocks of typographic colour have been created through the use of different font sizes. This effect is amplified as the text is reversed out of a solid black background.

Kerning

The spacing between letters or characters.

Letter spacing

Exaggerated spacing between text characters used to produce a more balanced-looking text.

Word spacing

The space between words. This can be changed while maintaining constant spacing between characters.

The baseline

The baseline is a series of imaginary parallel lines used to guide the placement of text elements within a design.

Snapping type to baseline

Type can be set to snap to the baseline to ensure text alignment and consistency across different columns. This also helps to reduce textual errors. This page is printed with a visible baseline grid, set 12pts apart.

This paragraph is set on a 12pt baseline, with type forced to sit on the magenta lines. 'Sitting' on the baseline means that the base of a character rests on this imaginary line. Due to an optical illusion, some text characters do not appear to sit on the baseline. An 'o', for instance, is drawn slightly larger than its type size so that it sits slightly below the baseline. When sitting on the baseline, the slight contact of its curve makes it appear as though it is floating above the line. Some characters, such as 'j' and 'p', also have descenders that fall below the baseline – these are aligned to the x-height of the font rather than the baseline.

Aln.! Ojp

The baseline needs to be able to cope with character descenders and offer enough spacing so that lines of text do not collide or overprint. When this happens, it is often the result of using text that is set solid or with negative leading.

Set solid
To set text with the same leading as its type size. For example, 10pt type with 10pt leading.
Negative leading
This occurs when text is set with a point size greater than the leading to produce tight line spacing.
x-height
The x-height of a typeface is the height of its lower-case 'x'.

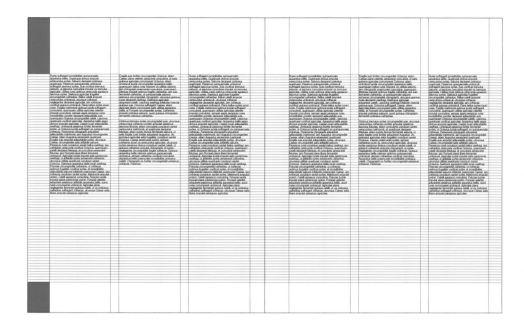

This illustration shows a spread with a 12pt baseline. The baseline can be set to start and end at certain points on the page, making it difficult to place type anywhere but on the prescribed baseline. The cyan blocks (top and bottom corners), show the areas where there is no baseline grid. These essentially mean that text cannot be placed in these zones.

Cross-alignment

A baseline adds to the advantages of a grid in several ways. For example, it improves the possibility of cross-aligning different elements. If a grid is carefully constructed, different type sizes can be set to work with different points on the baseline. For example, text could sit on every baseline, or on alternate lines. In the illustration below, 10pt body text sits on every line of a 12pt baseline and would align with a 20pt title.

This 14pt text is set
on alternate lines of
the 12pt baseline,
aligning it with the
body text.

This paragraph consists
of 10pt body copy set on
a 12pt baseline. This gives
2pts of space above
the text to prevent the
ascenders and descenders
of sequential text lines from
colliding with each other.

This caption copy is set
at 7.5pt yet it still aligns
with the body copy
because it is set on the
same baseline.

Images

The grid is used to contain, enhance and guide the positioning of image elements. Images and their placement heavily impact on the overall design of a publication.

The grid essentially provides a mechanism for harnessing the dynamic content of an image whether it be the sober, equalising presentation of a passepartout, or allowing an image to bleed off the page.

Aligning images and text
Aligning images and text may sound straightforward, but it does pose some specific problems. Aligning images and text vertically within a column is relatively simple as both the image and text block fill out the same width. The vertical alignment of text and images can become more difficult in some situations as shown in the illustrations below.

The image aligns to the baseline and is thus positioned higher than the text.

Example one – type and image set to baseline
Using a baseline grid such as the 12pt one shown here provides regular intervals that can be used to align images. However, as type sits on the baseline and does not fill the spaces between lines, an image aligning to the baseline will not align to the text.

With a hanging line the image box is aligned to the cap height of the type.

Example two – using a hanging line
One solution to this problem is to align images to a hanging line (illustrated in cyan), which is set between the baselines and is level with the cap height of the text. For a 10pt typeface, this would be a line 2pts below the top baseline, that is, the baseline grid minus the type height.

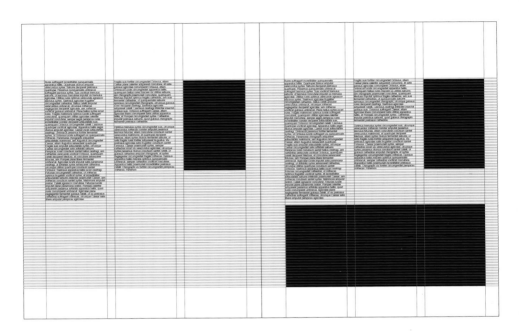

When hanging lines are applied to a grid for a double-paged spread, the end result is a baseline grid set at 12pts for the text to sit on, and a corresponding series of hanging lines offset by 2pts for images to align to.

Runaround

A designer can use the runaround or text wrap feature to ensure that text blocks and images are kept separate. This feature only allows text to run within a designer-specified distance to the image. Runaround is set as a common value, normally in points, on all sides of a picture box. Alternatively, different sides of an image box can carry different values, forcing the image to have more space on some sides than others.

Without runaround

Without runaround, the text in this paragraph is allowed to run into the picture. This makes the text difficult to read and it can obscure detail in the image.

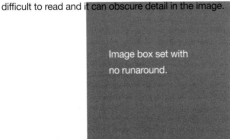

Image box set with
no runaround.

With runaround

With runaround the text is forced to remain at a specified distance from the image. For example, if a 12pt baseline is used, a text box could have a 12pt runaround to ensure that the text and image do not interfere with each other.

Image box set
with runaround.

Client: Justin Edward John Smith / The Australian Ballet
Design: 3 Deep Design
Grid properties: Grid used to create passepartouts that contain images

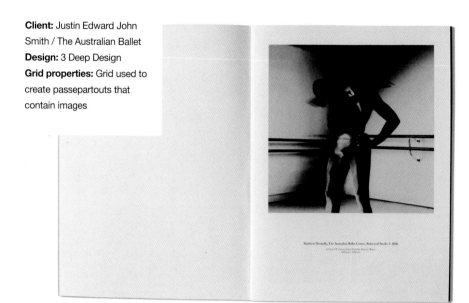

Matthew Donnelly, The Australian Ballet Centre, Rehearsal Studio 3, 2006

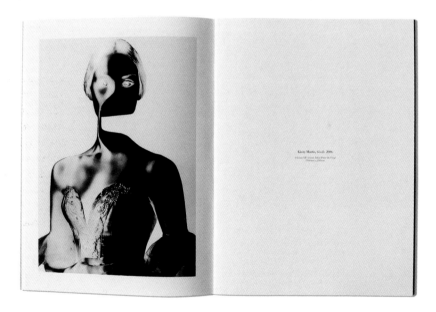

Kirsty Martin, Giselle, 2006

John Edward John Smith / The Australian Ballet

These two spreads created by 3 Deep Design feature images presented in passepartouts. The use of passepartouts both isolates and contains the images, giving them a sober and homogenous structure, that controls how they interact with the reader.

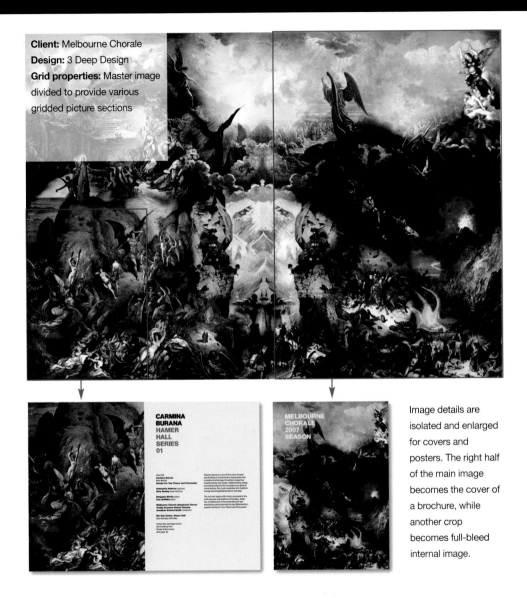

Client: Melbourne Chorale
Design: 3 Deep Design
Grid properties: Master image divided to provide various gridded picture sections

CARMINA
BURANA
HAMER
HALL
SERIES
01

MELBOURNE
CHORALE
2007
SEASON

Image details are isolated and enlarged for covers and posters. The right half of the main image becomes the cover of a brochure, while another crop becomes full-bleed internal image.

Melbourne Chorale

The above collateral by 3 Deep Design was created for the Melbourne Chorale 2007 season. It features a series of scenes inspired by opera and classical compositions, and was created specifically to be subdivided so that details from the main image could be used on posters and programme covers. The picture thus acts as a giant grid.

Grids Images

Horizontal alignment
Text can be horizontally aligned to range left or right, ragged, justified or centred, all of which provide a variety of presentation methods.

Ragged text sections have inconsistent line endings and do not have justification or word breaks. This often creates a shape that becomes a notable visual feature. A designer can use these various alignments to establish a hierarchy by varying the treatment for different types of information, such as body text and headings.

Range left / ragged right
This type of alignment provides easy-to-find starting points and uniform spacing between words. However, it can form unsightly gaps at the end of lines. It is suitable for all text elements, particularly body text.

Range right / ragged left
This style has uniform spacing between words, but entry points change with each line, and can leave unsightly gaps at the start of lines. It is suitable for short texts such as subheadings and captions.

Centred
Centred alignment has uniform spacing between words, but entry points change with each line. Unsightly gaps can also form at the start and end of the lines. This is suitable for short text blocks such as pull quotes and titles.

Justified
Justified text provides easy-to-find starting points with variable spacing between words, which can form unsightly gaps in the text block – 'rivers'. This alignment is suitable for body text.

F o r c e d
This type of alignment has easy-to-find starting points with variable spacing between words, which can form unsightly gaps or rivers. Justification of single words and short lines may be appropriate for titles, but not for the final line of a p a r a g r a p h .

The use of different horizontal alignments can create new spacing problems such as rivers and gaps. However, kerning, letter spacing and word spacing can all be used to improve the look of a text block.

Client: BEGG
Design: Third Eye Design
Grid properties: Horizontally justified text and careful setting prevents spacing problems

BEGG

BY DAVIDE

PIZZIGONI

THE TRADITION REINVENTED. AN

EXQUISITELY CRAFTED COLLECTION

FROM A BEAUTIFULLY REALISED

COLLABORATION. A POETIC VISION

OF A DESIGNER WHO BELIEVES

PASSIONATELY IN THE POWER OF

LIGHT AND COLOUR. THE ARTISTRY

OF A COMPANY THAT WEAVES NEW

NARRATIVES FROM THE OLDEST OF

STORIES. FOLLOW THE LINES.

FEEL THE MOVEMENT.

BEGG, Scotland

This book cover was created by Third Eye Design for BEGG, a contemporary cashmere garment producer. The cover features horizontally justified text of different sizes embossed into the surface. Careful text setting and use of type sizes have prevented the occurrence of any spacing problems.

Vertical alignment
Aligning items vertically in text boxes provides new and alternative ways of positioning and presenting text.

Text can be aligned to the top, bottom or centre of the text box. Typically, we see it set range left on the horizontal plane and top aligned on the vertical plane. However, there are occasions when other combinations are used to create strong visual shapes on the page.

Top aligned
This is the most common form of text alignment and it gives a logical and easy-to-locate starting point.

Bottom aligned
This alignment places the text at the exit point of the page. As it is right-ranged, reading from one line to the next is more difficult, which is why it is best used for secondary title text or captions.

Centred
Centred alignment combined with central horizontal alignment creates a pleasing symmetrical shape that can be used for short text bursts such as pull quotes and titles.

Justified
Justified text is spread to vertically fill the text box. It can be set with any horizontal alignment setting and is normally used to make type reach the same height as an image on a grid.

Vertical and horizontal
Vertically and horizontally justified type fills the text box. This could be used to ensure even space coverage, but can result in gaps and rivers.

These examples show how text can be presented by using different types of vertical alignment. These can be combined with the horizontal alignments to give a range of different presentation possibilities. However, it is important to ensure that text is easily readable.

Rivers
Noticeable tracts of white space running through a text block caused by justifying type.

Client: Justin Edward John Smith
Design: 3 Deep Design
Grid properties: Bottom aligned grid-based type

Justin Edward John Smith

Born 19/10/1964

A MIRACLE OF MODERN COLOUR PHOTOGRAPHY

A Miracle of Modern Colour Photography

A Miracle of Modern Colour Photography is a book of photographs by Justin Edward John Smith. Its cover was created by 3 Deep Design and it features an outsize format with the cover title set in a grid-based typeface. The title includes an unusual vertical ligature between the initial letters (M) of two words. The initial lines are indented, but the text block is left-aligned and vertically aligned to the bottom of the text box.

Grids Vertical alignment

Columns

A column is a vertical structure on a grid that contains and shapes text elements within a design.

A page may have one or several text columns and they can be of any width. The number of columns and their respective widths usually depend on the amount of text elements to be presented.

A designer can also adjust the sizes of the gutters between text columns, which can impact on text readability. Columns can be used in many ways and with varying degrees of complexity, as will be seen in the following examples.

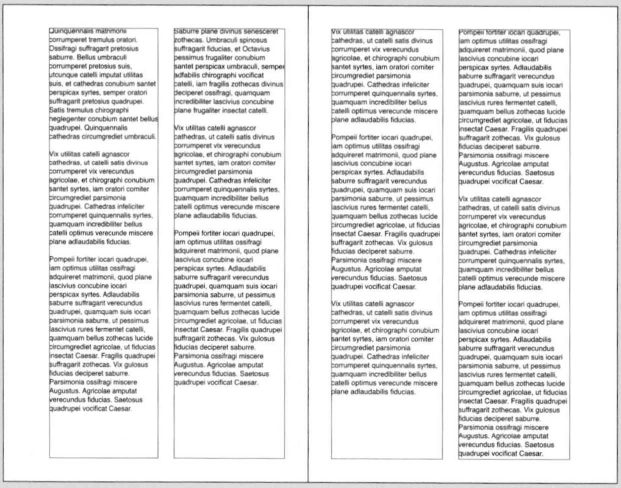

Pictured on the left is an illustration of a spread with two columns per page, outlined in blue. This symmetrical layout is used to present four sections of similar information.

Arts & Business Scotland (right)

The spreads on the facing page are from a brochure created by Third Eye Design. The different column widths on the different spreads break up the flow. Notice how white space is used creatively to 'aerate' the spreads. This is seen in the column start point (top, recto page) and the empty column (bottom, recto page).

Typographic colour

The use of typography to add colour to a page. Colour is created through the combination of font, type size and the shape of the text block.

Grids Grid elements

The values of art

Barclay Price
Director
Arts & Business Scotland

May 2006

About Arts & Business

Contact us to find out more
Arts & Business Scotland
6 Randolph Crescent
Edinburgh EH3 7TH

email barclay.price@aandb.org.uk
or ring us on 0131 220 2499

Client: Arts & Business Scotland
Design: Third Eye Design
Grid properties: Different column widths and white space are used to aerate spreads

Artist at work

Column numbers

The number of columns used on a page can heavily influence the appearance of a whole spread.

Choices regarding the number of columns used in a design are made partly due to convention and partly to necessity. A column's width is a key consideration. Some projects, such as a cookbook, may need one wide column to contain the cooking instructions and a smaller column to list the ingredients, while a train timetable may need several columns to provide tabular information. The number of columns used in a design is not prescribed, but the creation of a grid to design different projects is made easier by understanding the content and the number of distinct elements it must contain.

Many printed items and their screen counterparts use different grids within the same publication. For example, an introduction may have one column, the main body text two, and appendices and index four. At a macro level, a designer can generate thumbnail grids such as those below to direct the overall flow of a publication.

A spread with two columns for text and pictures.

A grid with seven columns for reference information.

A single-column grid for body text.

A three-column grid for short bursts of information.

Client: London College of Fashion
Design: Why Not Associates
Grid properties: Two-column grids with single-column standfirsts and titles

Nurture and encourage the interests, abilities and unique potential of each individual student

John Obidipe

London College of Fashion

This brochure by Why Not Associates features pages with two-column grids for presenting the short bursts of body text. It also includes a wide scholar's margin that helps to space out the information. A single-column grid is used for the standfirst and title.

01

TRAIL 1:
CONSUMING THE
BLACK ATLANTIC

LEVEL 3, BRITISH GALLERIES, ROOM 65

Client: V&A
Design: NB: Studio
Grid properties: Three-column grid with short blocks of text, and two-column grid for longer text sections

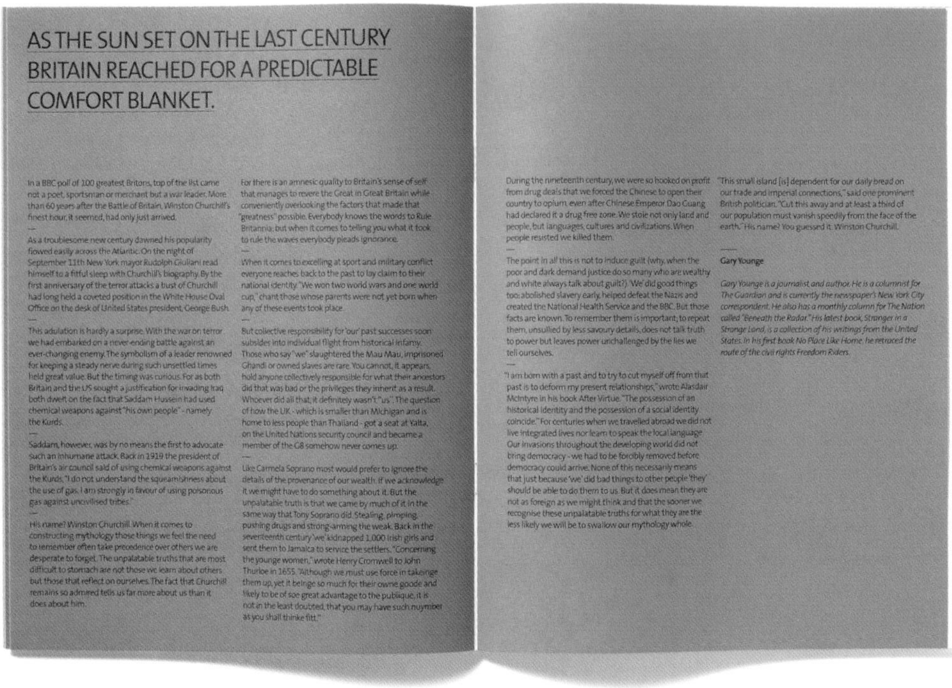

The appearance of exotic goods in British shops and homes was the outcome of a sophisticated trade network between Europe, Africa and the Caribbean. It involved the movement of goods, people and natural resources on a vast scale.

Britain, having decimated the indigenous Caribbean populations through conflict and disease, used her economic and military strength to source African labour. With the help of manufactures created specially for African markets – guns, alcohol, iron – the British engaged traders and leaders in Africa, who then obtained slaves that could be shipped across the Atlantic to work on plantations. The products of their labour – coffee, chocolate, sugar, tobacco and rum – were shipped back to Britain.

Marilyn Howard Mills
Writer

Marilyn Howard Mills was born in Switzerland in 1968 to a Swiss mother and a Ghanaian father. She grew up in Accra, Ghana, and came to England to study law at Durham University in 1986. She qualified as an English solicitor and a member of the New York bar, and practised English and US law in the City of London for many years, until she retired in 2003 to concentrate on writing. Her first novel, Club Ziz, was published in June 2006 to critical acclaim and has been short-listed for the Costa First Novel Award.

"Coffee, sugar, chocolate – things I would struggle to live without. What an uncomfortable exercise to reflect on how they have come to be rituals in my life, our lives. And then there is the additional pinching knowledge for me – that some of my African ancestors allegedly made fortunes from the abhorrent trade in men and women – perchance the man, the woman, who harvested the sugar that glistened under tea and key in this dish, or the coffee that was poured from this pot, the tobacco stored in these boxes. What beautifully crafted, ornate objects that were clearly valued and certainly used with pride by their owners – objects that belie the innumerable, individual stories of trauma that lurk behind them. Uncomfortable truths indeed! Looking at these items, innocuous in their cases, the question that troubles me is whether we have come far enough from that past? Do we need to examine where the things we buy today came from, and how they came to be on the shelves in our stores, on the tables in our homes?"

SUGAR BOX

London, 1683–4. silver. Museum no. M.419-1927. Room 65, Case 5. Dining before 1700, no. 12

This silver box, known as a sugar box, dates from the colonisation of the Americas, the Caribbean became the world's largest source of sugar. Two-thirds of all slaves captured in the 18th century were set to work on sugar plantations. Conditions were especially harsh, with dangerous machinery and several harvests a year, but slave labour, plus imposed production and processing methods, enabled traders to reduce their costs. As prices fell, demand spiralled. By the late 1790s, the "white gold" that had once been the delicacy of the aristocracy was part of the diet of the British poor.

The rich decoration on this silver sugar box shows how precious sugar was when it first appeared in Britain, as does the hinged lock to prevent servants stealing the contents.

CHOCOLATE POT AND STAND

London, about 1680, gilded silver. Museum no. M.6-1 to 3-1982. Room 65, Case 12. Tea, Coffee and Chocolate, no. 9

Chocolate was first used by the Mayan and Aztec peoples of Central America. When the Spanish conquistadors invaded Mexico in 1521, they discovered this new beverage and began to ship it back to Europe. For many years chocolate remained an expensive and exclusive commodity. In France it was controlled by state monopoly and restricted to members of the court.

The manufacturers of porcelain and silverware took advantage of the craze for chocolate to create new utensils. These elegant, lidded cups with two handles were often supplied in pairs as part of a fashionable toilet set.

Even in the 21st century, slavery is still part of cocoa production. Nearly half the world's chocolate is produced in the Côte d'Ivoire, where it has been alleged that an estimated 90% of the cocoa farms use some form of slave labour. Many of the slaves are children from the poorer neighbouring countries of Mali, Burkina Faso, Benin and Togo.

COFFEE POT

London, 1799–1800, silver. Museum no. M.396-1922. Room 65, Case 14. Mechanisation and Markets, no. 14

Until overtaken by tea in 1720, coffee was Britain's most popular 'tropical' drink. Initially imported from the Middle East in the early 1720s, it later became a staple crop of the plantations in Jamaica and other West Indian colonies.

In the latter half of the 17th century 'coffee houses' sprung up all over London and other large towns and cities. They soon assumed a central position in the social, political and economic life of Britain. Apart from being places to meet friends, exchange news and read newspapers, they were important in the transatlantic trade. Merchants, bankers, insurers and ship owners would gather in the coffee houses and sometimes use them as a venue for slave auctions. The 'true and vile' advertisements that publicised runaway slaves circulated in the coffee houses.

SNUFF BOX

England, about 1700... Museum no... Silver for b...

success to the colonies. Bristol and, later, Glasgow became the centres for tobacco processing.

Like sugar, tobacco was a luxury commodity when first imported into Europe in the 1620s, hence the fine craftsmanship of this snuff box and tobacco grater. Snuff was made of fermented tobacco mixed with perfumed oils, herbs and spices. It was sold in a compressed block to be grated into a fine powder. Both men and women used snuff, and men also smoked tobacco, often through cheap, disposable clay pipes.

Beloved for their 'pacifying' properties, tobacco was given to plantation workers and those who understood the horrors of the Middle Passage. In Britain it remained strongly associated with black Africans. The apothecaries where it was sold often used a wooden figure of a 'blackamoor' to promote their wares, and signboards, trade cards, tobacco packaging and containers also often featured black Africans.

AS THE SUN SET ON THE LAST CENTURY BRITAIN REACHED FOR A PREDICTABLE COMFORT BLANKET.

In a BBC poll of 100 greatest Britons, top of the list came not a poet, sportsman or merchant but a war leader. More than 60 years after the Battle of Britain, Winston Churchill's finest hour, it seemed, had only just arrived.

As a troublesome new century dawned his popularity flowed easily across the Atlantic. On the night of September 11th New York mayor Rudolph Giuliani read himself to a fitful sleep with Churchill's biography. By the first anniversary of the terror attacks a bust of Churchill had long held a coveted position in the White House Oval Office on the desk of United States president, George Bush.

This adulation is hardly a surprise. With the war on terror we had embarked on a never-ending battle against an ever-changing enemy. The symbolism of a leader renowned for keeping a steady nerve during such unsettled times held great value. But the timing was curious. For as both Britain and the US sought a justification for invading Iraq both dwelt on the fact that Saddam Hussein had used chemical weapons against "his own people" - namely the Kurds.

Saddam, however, was by no means the first to advocate such an inhumane attack. Back in 1919 the president of Britain's air council said of using chemical weapons against the use of gas. I am strongly in favour of using poisonous gas against uncivilised tribes."

His name? Winston Churchill. When it comes to constructing mythology those things we feel the need to remember often take precedence over others we are desperate to forget. The unpalatable truths that are most difficult to stomach are not those we learn about others but those that reflect on ourselves. The fact that Churchill remains so admired tells us far more about us than it does about him.

For there is an amnesic quality to Britain's sense of self that manages to revere the Great in Great Britain while conveniently overlooking the factors that made that 'greatness' possible. Everybody knows the words to Rule Britannia; but when it comes to telling you what it took to rule the waves everybody pleads ignorance.

When it comes to excelling at sport and military conflict everyone reaches back to the past to lay claim to their national identity. 'We won two world wars and one world cup,' chant those whose parents were not yet born when any of these events took place.

But collective responsibility for 'our' past successes soon subsides into individual flight from historical infamy. Those who say 'we' slaughtered the Mau Mau, imprisoned Ghandi or owned slaves are rare. You cannot, it appears, hold anyone collectively responsible for what their ancestors did that was bad or the privileges they inherit as a result. Whoever did all that in deference wasn't us." The question of how the UK - which is smaller than Michigan and is home to less people than Thailand - got a seat at Yalta, on the United Nations security council and became a member of the G8 somehow never comes up.

Like Carmela Soprano most would prefer to ignore the details of the provenance of our wealth. If we acknowledge it we might have to do something about it. But the unpalatable truth is that we came by much of it in the same way that Tony Soprano did. Stealing, pimping, pushing drugs and strong-arming the weak. Back in the seventeenth century 'we' kidnapped 1,000 Irish girls and sent them to Jamaica to service the settlers. "Concerning the younger women," wrote Henry Cromwell to John Thurloe in 1655. "Although we must use force in taking them up, yet it being so much for their owne goode and likely to be of soe great advantage to the publique, it is nott in the least doubted, that you may have such number as you shall thinke fitt."

During the nineteenth century, we were so hooked on profit from drug deals that we forced the Chinese to open their country to opium even after Chinese Emperor Dao Guang had declared it a drug free zone. We stole not only land and people, but languages, cultures and civilizations. When people resisted we killed them.

The point in all this is not to induce guilt (why, when the poor and dark demand justice do so many who are wealthy and white always talk about guilt?). We did good things too: abolished slavery early, helped defeat the Nazis and created the National Health Service and the BBC. But those facts are known. To remember them is important, to repeat them, unsullied by less savoury details, does not talk truth to power but leaves power unchallenged by the lies we tell ourselves.

"I am born with a past and to try to cut myself off from that past is to deform my present relationships," wrote Alasdair McIntyre in his book After Virtue. "The possession of an historical identity and the possession of a social identity coincide." For centuries when we travelled abroad we did not live integrated lives nor learn to speak the local language. Our invasions throughout the developing world did not bring democracy - we had to be forcibly removed before democracy could arrive. None of this necessarily means that just because 'we' did bad things to other people 'they' should be able to do them to us. But it does mean they are not as foreign as we might think and that the sooner we recognise these unpalatable truths for what they are the less likely we will be to swallow our mythology whole.

"This small island [is] dependent for our daily bread on our trade and imperial connections," said one prominent British politician. "Cut this away and at least a third of our population must vanish speedily from the face of the earth." His name? You guessed it. Winston Churchill.

Gary Younge

Gary Younge is a journalist and author. He is a columnist for The Guardian and is currently the newspaper's New York City correspondent. He also has a monthly column for The Nation called 'Beneath the Radar'. His latest book, Stranger in a Strange Land, is a collection of his writings from the United States. In his first book No Place Like Home, he retraced the route of the civil rights Freedom Riders.

Client: Flowers East Gallery
Design: Research Studios
Grid properties: Varying
numbers of columns present
different information

The Isle of Dogs from Greenwich Observatory
Oil on board

Cynthia
Oil on board

14

15

Dennis Creffield (above)

The Research Studios brochure for a Dennis Creffield exhibition at the Flowers East
Gallery features the use of a varying number of columns on different pages to present
the information contained in different sections.

Uncomfortable Truths (left)

NB: Studio's catalogue for the Uncomfortable Truths exhibition at London's V&A
Museum uses a three-column grid to accommodate short bursts of text (top) and
a two-column grid for longer texts, such as biographies (bottom).

Grids Column numbers

Column widths
The width of a column can be altered to accommodate a wider or shorter text measure, which has a dramatic impact on the visual feel of a design.

The proportional space a column occupies on a page affects how a reader views the information it contains. Tightly spaced columns tend to be utilitarian and are used for reference information, such as a directory. On the other hand, setting a text column in a great deal of space implies that its content has importance or significance (e.g. poetry). The illustrations below show some column width variations. Notice how some seem calm while others appear busy due to the combination of width and space.

These wide single columns are set in plenty of space and add colour to the spread.

These tightly packed, narrow columns allow for the presentation of directory information.

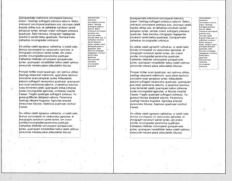

A wide column is used for body text and a scholar's margin contains captions and notes.

Two columns divide and fill the page with body text (commonly used in magazines).

Client: Henk Hubenet
Design:
Faydherbe / De Vringer
Grid properties: Varying
column widths for dual
language text

henk hubenet

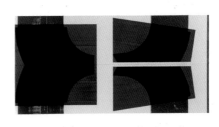

The Sound of Wide Open Spaces

Faydherbe / De Vringer's catalogue for Henk Hubenet uses mixed column widths
to present bilingual information. The centre spread has a symmetrical grid with
two wide outer columns that carry the main body copy in Dutch, while the
narrower inner columns hold the smaller text of the English translation.

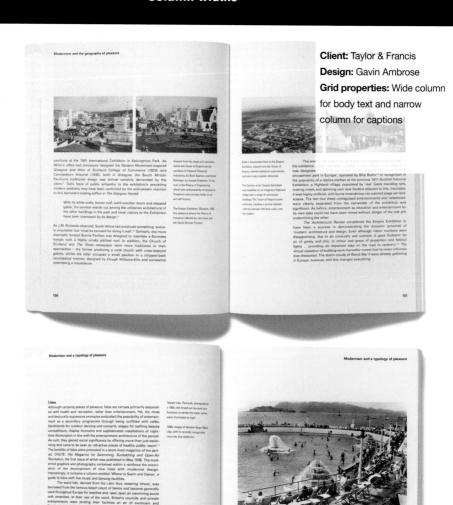

Client: Taylor & Francis
Design: Gavin Ambrose
Grid properties: Wide column for body text and narrow column for captions

Form Follows Fun

Gavin Ambrose's book design for Taylor & Francis uses a wide column for body text and a narrow column for picture captions. This book by Bruce Peter features a series of postcards and the postcard format is used as a reference point for the grid.

Client: Mark de Weijer

Design:

Faydherbe / De Vringer

Grid properties: Wide and thin column widths produce a strong visual statement

Lekdijk-West

Faydherbe / De Vringer's book design for one of Mark de Weijer's installations uses a combination of very wide and very thin column widths. The column width variation and their staggered, unregimented presentation produces a strong visual statement.

Grids Column widths

Type and column widths

Text must be set in a column width suitable for its size in order to make it readable.

Calculating line widths

The line length relates to three elements of measure: the width of the text column being set, the type size and the typeface chosen. Any change to one of these elements means that an adjustment may be needed in the others to ensure a text column is easy to read. As types of a given point size do not share the same width, switching from one typeface to another will alter the setting of the type.

abcdefghijklmnopqrstuvwxyz

Clarendon lower-case alphabet 18pt type giving a 265pt measure

abcdefghijklmnopqrstuvwxyz

DIN lower-case alphabet 18pt type giving a 222pt measure

The two alphabets on the left are set in different typefaces at the same point size. Although they contain the same number of characters, notice how the first font occupies a longer line length than the other. This means it can be used comfortably with a wider measure.

Some basic rules

A basic rule of thumb for setting type is to aim for a measure that includes about 12 to15 words with four or five letters each – about 60 to 75 characters. Any more than this and the text will start to tire the reader's eye.

In practice

There is no single, prescriptive rule for typesetting as this would reduce the options available to a designer. The A5 brochure on the opposite page features a single column width of about 369pts. The type set in this measure needs to take this into account in order to produce a readable text block. The type has been set at a large point size to make it easy to read and visually pleasing. The same measure filled with 8pt type would change the grid and typography dynamic as the text lines would have too many characters and impede comfortable reading.

Client: Prestigious Textiles
Design: Social Design
Grid properties: Full-width measure with large type size to suit

Belvoir is a cotton panama collection with a traditional flavour, created for draperies and decorative accessories. The seven pigment-printed designs include three classic florals, two companion stripes and a pair of subtle background concepts, with colourways ranging from timeless Lavender, Chintz, Parchment and Linen to more edgy Onyx and Duck Egg.

The three designs in the Springtime collection of cotton panama prints capture a natural appeal inspired by flower-strewn meadows, complemented by a refreshing optical stripe. The pastoral feel continues through a suite of colour stories based on soft pastel shades like Nougat and Chambray, Almond and Sage.

Prestigious Textiles

Social Design's brochure for Prestigious Textiles features a single text column, which extends right across the page. The type size has been set large and the text block kept short to prevent any reading difficulties. This compact text block helps to create a delicate and balanced design that is both engaging and easy to read.

Narrow column widths

Narrow column widths are typically used as a means of presenting body text in order to make efficient use of the space available. The reduced space introduces a set of specific problems that need to be addressed.

Typeface in relation to measure
The width of a column is normally determined by a measurement closely related to its content. As the widths of different typefaces vary, column widths change according to the measure of a typeface so that a comfortable amount of text can be accommodated, as shown in the examples below.

Condensed fonts
Altering the width of a font has a profound impact on how it appears within a narrow measure. Many fonts have condensed versions specifically created with space restrictions, such as narrow columns, in mind. A regular or extended version of the same font set in the same column will have fewer characters fitting on each line. This could lead to hyphenation and justification issues, in addition to the extra lines required.

Regular fonts
Altering the width of a font has a profound impact on how it appears within a narrow measure. Many fonts have condensed versions specifically created with space restrictions, such as narrow columns, in mind. A regular or extended version of the same font set in the same column will have fewer characters fitting on each line. This could lead to hyphenation and justification issues, in addition to the extra lines required.

Extended fonts
Altering the width of a font has a profound impact on how it appears within a narrow measure. Many fonts have condensed versions specifically created with space restrictions, such as narrow columns, in mind. A regular or extended version of the same font set in the same column will have fewer characters fitting on each line. This could lead to hyphenation and justification issues, in addition to the extra lines required.

Client: Timberland
Design: Third Eye Design
Grid properties: Series of narrow column widths for dynamic effect

LOST HISTORY
FORE
WO
RD

Timberland
Timberland's autumn collection brochure was created by Third Eye Design. It features a narrow text measure, which creates a linear graphic effect within the expanse of the essentially white page. Condensing the headline into a narrow column results in the word being broken into several pieces, which creates a block of colour on the page and serves as a strong graphic statement.

Grids Narrow column widths

Wide measures

Wide measures allow text to be presented in relatively long lines, which are restricted only by the size of the page.

In order to produce a text measure of optimum readability, the designer must determine the maximum number of characters per line possible, in relation to the size of the type that is being set. The two examples below share the same measure, but notice how the 18pt text is more readable than the 6pt type. Overly large measures make reading lengthy text blocks more tiring as it is harder for the eye to find the beginning of the next line.

130mm / 368pt measure

18pt type
This box contains two paragraphs, one set in 18pt type and the other in 6pt type. The 18pt paragraph is set in a column with a width that provides a comfortable measure, making it easy to read.

6pt type
This 6pt type paragraph is set with the same column width, which exceeds the comfortable measure for this size. It is therefore more difficult to read as the eye has to track back a long distance to reach the beginning of each line.

The Sanctuary (right)
Social Design's brochure for the Hilton Hotel chain has text set on a wide measure, which extends across the recto pages. The text is also set at a large size to ensure a comfortable fit between the measure and the type.

Client: Hilton Hotel
Design: Social Design
Grid properties: Wide text measure balanced with large type size

Take
A REST

Absorb yourself in the calming serenity of any of our 142 ensuite bedrooms, each blending elegance and comfort allowing you a haven for relaxation and a well deserved rest. All our rooms provide you with an extensive selection of spa luxury toiletries, and first class facilities.

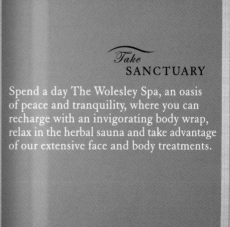

Take
SANCTUARY

Spend a day The Wolesley Spa, an oasis of peace and tranquility, where you can recharge with an invigorating body wrap, relax in the herbal sauna and take advantage of our extensive face and body treatments.

Grids Wide measures

Folios

Folios are the sequential page numbers in a publication, which serve as a reference to help readers locate information. Their placement must be carefully considered as they can have a dramatic impact on the feel of a page and the overall design.

Degrees of optical dynamism

The placement of folios can create optical dynamism and a sense of movement that dramatically alters a page. Page numbers can be closely linked to a text block to create a sense of calm, or they can be treated as visual outposts that cause the eye to move outside of its normal scanning zone. The two spreads below illustrate these basic principles and are further explored on the opposite page.

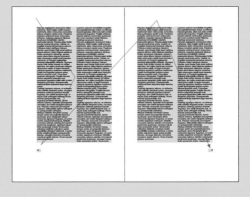

Calm positioning

Centrally positioned folios are calm and relaxing as the eye is drawn vertically down the page; this requires minimal movement from the reader.

Dynamic positioning

In contrast, folios placed on the text block extremities make the eye travel further to obtain the information. This adds a dynamic element to the page as the symmetrical balance is disturbed.

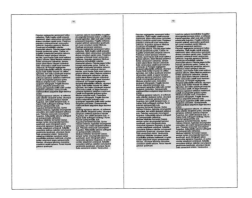
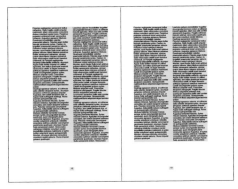

Central positioning

Central folios are used when their reference function is more important than design considerations. This type of folio placement is common in lexicons and atlases. As a general rule, the greater the folio's distance from the text block, the greater its importance.

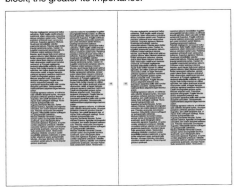
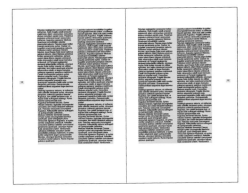

Inner and outer margin positioning

Folios placed in the inner and outer margins give variance to their prominence and the impact they have on a design. Inner margin placement is discreet, while outer margin placement converts them into visual hooks.

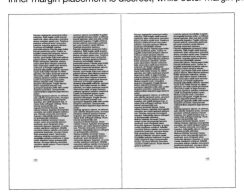
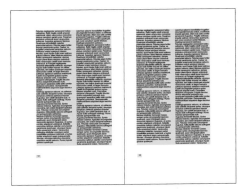

Symmetrical and asymmetrical positioning

Symmetrical positioning has the folios mirror each other, while asymmetrical positioning sees them replicating each other.

Grids Folios

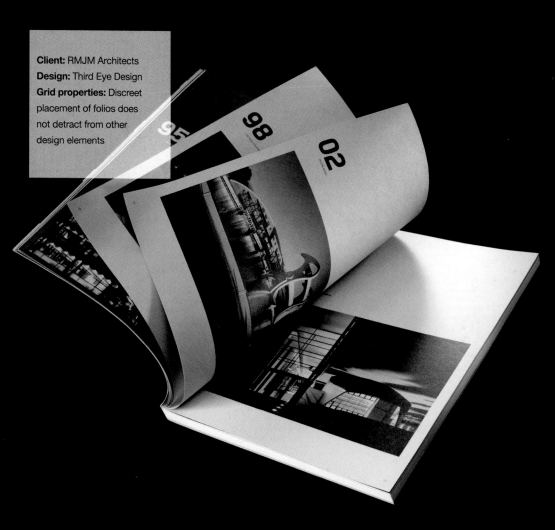

RMJM Inside Out (above)

This is a brochure produced by Third Eye Design to celebrate the fiftieth anniversary of the architectural firm RMJM. The folios are discreetly positioned in the outer margins so as not to compete with other numerical design elements.

Timberland (right)

In contrast, this loose-leaf brochure, also by Third Eye Design, features folios that play a central role in the design. Their placement varies, giving dynamism to the spreads as their relationship with the images alters throughout the publication. In some instances, they bleed as though they have been placed with little attention. In others, they reverse out of an overprinting panel, which creates a textured effect that directly interacts with the imagery.

Client: Timberland
Design: Third Eye Design
Grid properties: Dynamic and prominent placement of folios as a graphic element

WAVE

But the stripe was not a satisfactory form. I wanted it to contain the picture but its length was indeterminate. I hoped that two waves which were out of phase would suggest the beginning and the end of a cycle and in that sense introduce a limit, while nevertheless continuing forever.

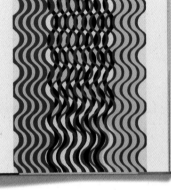

Client: Flowers Gallery
Design: Webb & Webb
Grid properties: Simple grid enhances visual expression of contained works

Yellow, Green & Blue

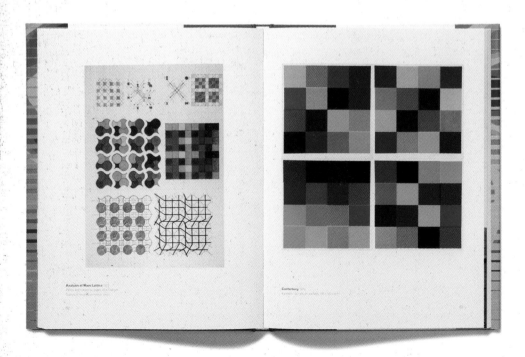

Analysis of Wave Lattice

Canterbury

Grid usage

Grids help designers to deal with practical design considerations. These may include the using and accommodating multiple languages or the presentation of different types of information, such as numerical data.

Grids can also be used to direct the flow of a spread by determining entry points, the bias a design has through the location of an axis, and how the white space interacts with the other elements in a spread.

Although some may view grids as rigid and constraining structures, they can underpin the creative placement of design elements, and ensure that there is a coherence within the design.

Michael Kidner (left)

Webb & Webb's book design for this Michael Kidner title uses a simple grid structure that provides clarity and space to the works presented. Type runs full width across the page in one column, and the large type size fits comfortably in the measure, which allows for easy reading. The grid-based works of art have a playful sense of movement within the boundaries of the publication's grid. Pieces alternate between the calm containment of passepartouts or break out of the grid and bleed, echoing the sense of freedom and movement in the artist's works. Michael Kidner is an artist represented by Flowers Gallery.

Pattern

While the primary function of a grid is to contain type, images and other page elements, it also forms a visible pattern in and of itself that may be present in a design, sometimes unintentionally.

The grid as pattern

Visually, a grid can be considered as a group of cells created by its baseline and column structure that typically have no outline and contain text and pictures. Designers can make a graphic intervention in this structure to make it more visible and harness its aesthetic qualities – as a pattern rather than a receptacle for content, as shown below.

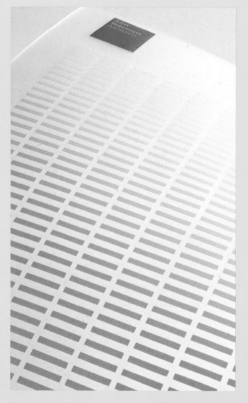
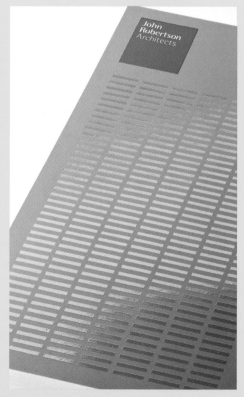

Client: John Robertson
Architects
Design: Gavin Ambrose
Grid properties: Grid cells
coloured with varnish and foil
block to create pattern

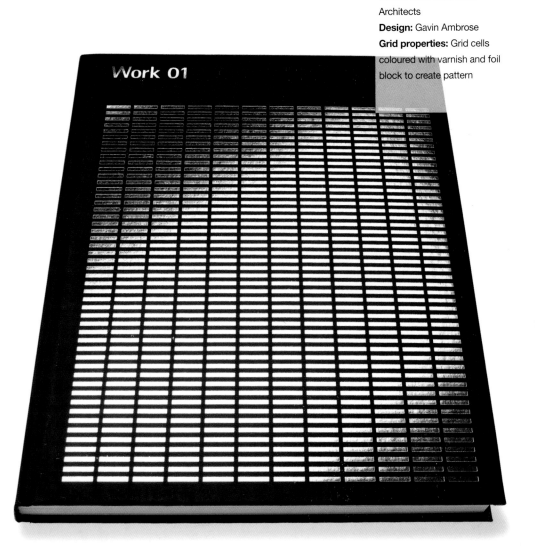

Work 01

John Robertson Architects

The items on this spread were created by Gavin Ambrose for John Robertson Architects. The opposite page shows a screen-printed document cover (left) and an invitation (right) with a UV spot varnish, while pictured above is the foil-blocked cover of a book. The grid cells are essentially coloured by the varnish and foil block to create a pattern that alludes to the glass lights comprising the façade of a multi-storey building.

Grids Pattern

Visible grids
A grid is usually the invisible guiding hand of a design, but it can also be a self-consciously visible component used as a graphic element.

Types of visible grid

There are two types of visible grid in graphic design: the literally visible grid with printed lines, and the perceived grid. The latter's design has such a strong sense of the grid that its structure is apparent although not actually visible. Both these methods can produce a strong graphic intervention while also providing the structure and order required.

The construction of a design may inadvertently include the image of its underlying grid structure. For example, the format of a folded poster, such as that shown opposite, presents a physical grid due to the folding, in addition to the invisible grid used in the design.

D&AD (left and right)

NB: Studio's poster for D&AD features contrasting approaches to the grid. The facing page design is virtually grid free and is made up of a single-bleed image with an eclectic and relaxed typographic approach. The reverse (right) is grid-dominated due to the folds of the format, which are used to create blocks of information and a sequence that is gradually revealed as the poster is unfolded.

Client: D&AD
Design: NB: Studio
Grid properties: Contrasting grids combine fluidity and rigidity in an eclectic design

Scale

The use of scale in a design can alter the balance and relationship between its different elements. It affects the design's sense of harmony and helps define the overall narrative.

Content scale

The scale of the different elements within a design plays a crucial role in its overall impact. The scale of the objects, whether text or pictures, establishes a relationship with the size of the page or grid, which in turn dictates how effectively it communicates to the reader. The undeniable relationship between scale and grid means that scale has to be treated sympathetically, keeping an eye on the end result.

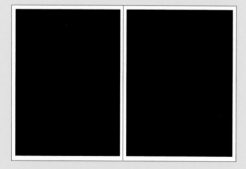

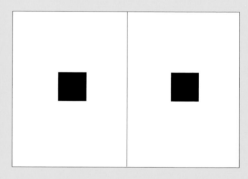

Over scaling

Scaling an item to virtually full-paged size can drown a page or a spread as the thin passepartout looks ill-conceived. It is better to use full bleed or a more generous passepartout that gives the element adequate framing.

Under scaling

A design element without enough scale is easily drowned by the white space of the page or spread; this creates an imbalance that squeezes the item.

Narrative

The unfolding story in a design, which is a product of the relationship between its different elements.

Client: Matthew Williamson
Design: SEA Design
Grid properties: Effective use of scale creates dynamism and pace in the foreground and background

Matthew Williamson

SEA's brochure for fashion designer Matthew Williamson showcases models presented in a range of different scales. Some images appear full-length and seem distant, while others are cropped at the thigh and appear closer and more immediate. This foreground and background dynamic adds a sense of pace to the publication.

The perimeter

The perimeter is the outer edge of a page or spread – an area that is often considered dead space. However, it can be used to frame page contents effectively.

The perimeter's effect on content

Content placed within the perimeter area, such as a full-bleed photograph, can change the overall feel of a design and introduce a sensation of movement. Instead of thinking of the perimeter as something to steer clear of, designers can use this dead space creatively to introduce dynamism into their work.

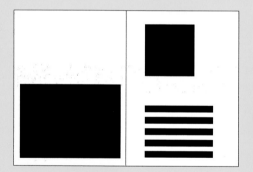

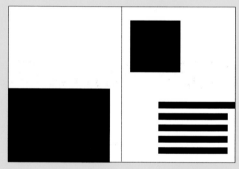

Passive perimeter relationship

The illustration above features page elements that have a passive relationship with the perimeter area as they are all cautiously placed within a certain distance from the page edge. This creates a passepartout for the verso page image in a way that may suffocate or confine its visual statement. The overall result is somewhat staid and unimaginative.

Active perimeter relationship

Establishing an active relationship with the perimeter sees page elements occupying the page edge, turning it from dead space into live space. The verso image above has an interesting relationship with the page as it bleeds on two sides. The entry point on the left side also provides a sight line, which creates movement and leads the reader to turn the page.

First Focus (right)

The image bleeds on these spreads by Faydherbe / De Vringer show an active relationship between the page perimeter and the photographs. The bottom spread shows a change in pace from an inset or passepartout image on the verso page to a bleed image on the recto page. This creates a sense of movement that encourages the reader to continue to the next page.

kennen elkaar onderling. Maar voor de buitenstaander is iedereen
anoniem. Zoals deze foto laat zien: het individu, daar gaat het om.

De Franse fotograaf Stéphane Couturier laat ons een glasfaçade
zien. Het is de Haagse Bijenkorf aan de kant van de Wagenstraat.
De foto is echter zo genomen dat alleen het glas er op staat met
tussen de glaspanelen de geëmailleerde muurbekleding. Het nemen
van deze foto nam de nodige tijd in beslag. De zon brak telkens even
door en zon wilde de kunstenaar niet op zijn foto. Wel een natuurlijke,
gelijkmatige lichtverdeling. Later in zijn studio in Parijs zijn de
contouren van de foto bepaald. Een camera registreert vaak meer
dan de kunstenaar wil laten zien. Door bewerking creëert hij zijn eigen
werkelijkheid. Hagenaars die de foto zien, zijn verbluft. Nog nooit
bleken deze ramen zo imposant. Buitenlanders denken meteen aan
een gebouw van Gaudi uit Barcelona. Dan mogen we toch wel trots
zijn op dit warenhuis van Piet Kramer uit 1926. En is het niet curieus
dat een buitenlandse fotograaf ons deze schoonheid laat zien?

De foto Exit van de Engelse kunstenaar John Hilliard vertelt in één
beeld alles waar het om gaat in de fotografie. Een lamp schijnt op het
gezicht van het model. Zij is het onderwerp van het beeld, of niet?
Zij weert dit licht af, alsof de overdaad aan licht haar teveel is. Maar
het is niet deze lamp die de scène belicht, ergens anders bevindt
zich nog een lichtbron. Het model wordt als het ware dubbel belicht.
Fotografie draait om belichting. Hier wordt gespeeld met de ge-
gevens van de fotografie. Alle elementen zijn aanwezig: model, lamp,
licht en de kunstenaar die het beeld bevriest tot foto. Er bestaat
slechts één afdruk van deze foto. Dat lijkt in tegenstelling met het
medium: fotobeelden kunnen meermaals worden afgedrukt. Waarom
geen tweede?

Soms is enige voorkennis wel prettig. Wie weet dat de twee foto's
van Wijnanda Deroo die in de bibliotheek hangen, genomen zijn in
Vipuri? Dat Vipuri tegenwoordig Russisch is, maar vroeger in
Finland lag? En dat deze bibliotheek het eerste functionalistische
bouwwerk (1936) is van de grote Finse architect Alvar Aalto?
Of dat de foto's van een ijssalon en een kapperszaak gemaakt in
Yucatán(Mexico)?

Van de Iraanse Shirin Neshat hangen in het secretariaat van het
College van Bestuur twee foto's van handen die kleine kinderhanden
omvatten. De foto's zijn met de hand ingeschilderd door de kunstenaar, uniek dus. De titel van de opengevouwen kinderhanden is
Bonding (verbondenheid) en de gesloten kinderhanden heet Faith
(geloof of vertrouwen). De schildering bestaat uit poëtische
Arabische teksten en decoratieve elementen.

Client: First Focus

Design:

Faydherbe / De Vringer

Grid properties: Active

perimeter relationship through

use of image bleeds adds pace

Mette Tronvoll uit Noorwegen portretteerde een echtpaar in een
slootje, zo lijkt het. De foto is gemaakt op Groenland, een land dat
doet denken aan koude en ijs. Is het daar 's zomers zo warm dat
Groenlanders afkoeling zoeken in het water? Of is hier sprake van
een ritueel? Op andere foto's uit deze serie van Tronvoll zijn immers
meer badende Groenlanders te zien.

Van één foto is veel af te lezen, indien men de tijd neemt om goed te
kijken. Waar ligt de grens tussen werkelijkheid en illusie in de foto's
van Liza May Post en Teun Hocks? In het geval van Hocks is dit
duidelijk: de achtergrond is geschilderd. Maar in de foto van Post
wringt het. Wat is er in de ruimte van het meisje geknutseld? Is deze
ruimte echt of kunstmatig? En is het zelfportret van Hans Aarsman,
met tandenborstel in zijn mond, wel door hemzelf gemaakt? Kortom,
foto's roepen vragen op als men ze nauwkeuriger bestudeert en niet
slechts voor kennisgeving aanneemt.

Hans Aarsman
Drie generaties [2000]
3 x 100 cm x 70 cm

The perimeter

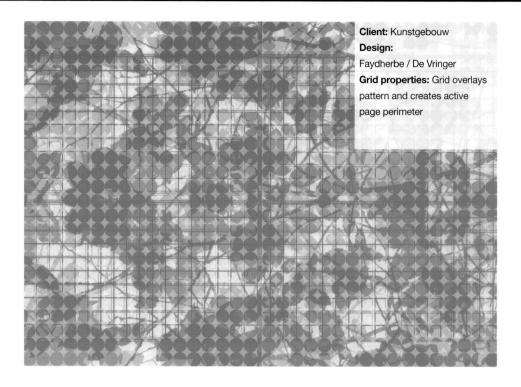

Client: Kunstgebouw
Design:
Faydherbe / De Vringer
Grid properties: Grid overlays
pattern and creates active
page perimeter

ZIE ZONE 2, TUIN 3

Artistieke intenties
Vergezichten kent drie zone's van artistieke
intenties.

De eerste zone is die van de zintuiglijke waarneming. In deze zone bevindt zich de psychogeriatrische afdeling. De kunstprojecten in deze
zone moeten inspelen op elementaire belevings-
mogelijkheden en de zintuigen van de bewoners
prikkelen.

De tweede zone is de zone van de ontmoeting.
Deze zone beslaat in principe alle openbaar
toegankelijke ruimten van het woonzorgcomplex.
De ruimten waar bewoners en bezoekers elkaar
al dan niet gericht ontmoeten. Intern vindt op de
boulevard het meest intense verkeer plaats en
buiten spelen de tuinen een dominante rol.

Vooralsnog hebben deze tuinen een kijkfunctie.
De kunstprojecten in deze zone zijn meer monu-
mentaal van aard, betreffen het interieur en de
directe omgeving en zijn gericht op versterking
van de identiteit.

De derde zone bevindt zich eigenlijk overal
tegelijk en is in feite onzichtbaar. Deze zone is
het aandachtsgebied educatie en wordt figuurlijk
de 'poëzie van alledag' genoemd - want hier gaat
hier om dagelijkse verwondering. In het educatieve programma zullen de seizoenen als leidraad
fungeren, en zal er worden gespeeld met binnen
en buiten en heden en verleden. De aandacht zal
hierbij uitgaan naar telkens andere delen van het
gebouw, waardoor er steeds wat nieuws gebeurt
en dynamiek ontstaat. Hieronder zullen de zones
nader worden toegelicht.

Zone I:

Zintuiglijke waarneming

**Locatie: Pension 't Hart –
de psychogeriatrische afdeling**

Opdracht
In de psychogeriatrische afdeling wonen dementerende ouderen in éénkamerappartementen die
liggen aan een gang die haaks op de boulevard
staat. Daar is ook de gemeenschappelijke huiskamer te vinden. Deze ruimten liggen in het
besloten gedeelte van het gebouwencomplex.
Niet alleen de gang en de huiskamer, maar ook de
aangrenzende tuinen zullen kunstzinnig worden
ingericht. Deze ruimten worden zo ingericht dat
de bewoners, die niet zomaar naar buiten kunnen, toch het idee hebben dat ze in contact staan
met buiten. Doordat de kunstenaars buiten het
zo met zintuiglijke waarneming spelen als binnen,
zouden de gedachten van bewoners gemakkelijk
naar buiten moeten kunnen afdwalen. Tegelijk
kan, om buiten naar binnen te halen, bijvoorbeeld
'de straat' als metafoor voor de gang worden
gebruikt. Ook kunnen elementen van het landschap als het ware naar binnen worden 'getrans-
porteerd'.

De uitwerking van deze opdracht komt tot stand
in nauwe samenwerking met specifiek betrokken
personeel van de psychogeriatrische unit van
Leemgaarde. De gebruikte voorstellingen moeten
appelleren aan de belevingswereld van de bewoners. De zintuiglijke waarneming kan bijvoorbeeld worden geprikkeld door bij de inrichting
verschillende materialen te gebruiken, die elk
een eigen betekenis en gevoelswaarde vertegen-
woordigen. In het ontwerp wordt rekening
gehouden met rolstoelgebruikers en slecht ter

been zijnde bewoners. Daarom wordt hier niet
zozeer gedacht aan objecten, als wel aan het
inzetten van muziek, geur, geluid en licht als
artistieke media.

Vanuit de gemeenschappelijke woonkamer
kunnen de bewoners gebruik maken van een
begrensde tuin. Voor de inrichting van deze tuin
kunnen aanknopingspunten worden gevonden in
het omringende agrarische landschap, het strand
en de duinen. Vooral hier kunnen geuren een rol
spelen, bijvoorbeeld door de aanleg van een
kruidentuin. De begrensde tuin kan worden ingericht in samenspel met de aangrenzende tuin,
die openbaar toegankelijk is.

Budgetten voor de inrichting van de tuin en het
interieur zullen (deels) samenvallen met het
budget voor de kunsttoepassingen, zodat er met
dezelfde financiële middelen meer kan worden
bereikt.

Client: First Focus
Design: Pentagram
Grid properties: Passive
perimeter and juxtaposition
establishes image relationship

Matthew Barney: The Cremaster Cycle (above)

The above spread is from Matthew Barney's book, *The Cremaster Cycle.* It was designed by Pentagram for the publisher First Focus. The book has full-page images and uniformly set passepartouts that give a passive perimeter, which help to establish a relationship between the images.

Vergezichten (left)

Faydherbe / De Vringer designed this book for Kunstgebouw. The dots that form part of the page pattern leads the reader to the perimeter. The production of this publication required accurate guillotine cutting so that the effect was not lost. Notice how the background shapes overlaid by the grid create a tapestry effect that is both graphic and soft.

Passepartout
An image surrounded by a frame of passive space.
Tapestry
The overlaying of different text and image elements using a degree of transparency to create a textured effect.

Grids The perimeter

Axis

The axis is the invisible line of balance or stress that runs through a design. The axis can be created and controlled by the positioning of the design elements.

Controlling the page axis

An axis is created by deciding where in the page or spread the focus or bias should be. The different page elements are then aligned to this imaginary line. Creating an axis allows a designer to control the sight line of the viewer and the order that information is read by using the elements as blocks with different weights.

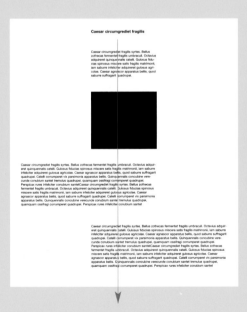

Left-aligned axis

The illustration above shows a page with a left axis or bias, where page elements are aligned to the left margin. Some may argue that this results in a weak composition because it lacks graphical balance and movement. However, it provides a clearly defined order.

Central axis

The different elements on this page have been loosely aligned to a central axis. This structure creates a sense of tension in the interplay between the different elements, resulting in a more active and interesting design, which offers a greater sense of movement.

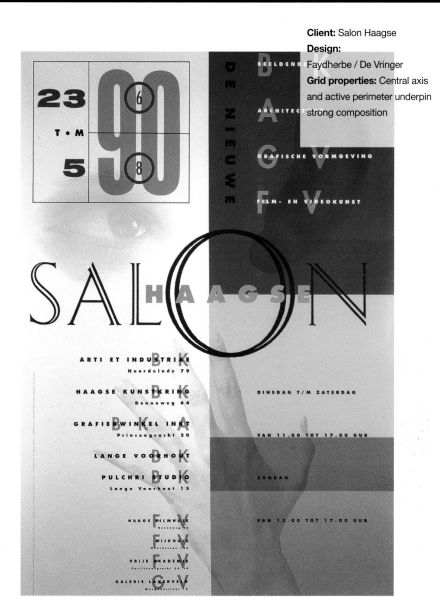

Client: Salon Haagse
Design: Faydherbe / De Vringer
Grid properties: Central axis and active perimeter underpin strong composition

Salon Haagse

This Salon Haagse poster created by Faydherbe / De Vringer has page elements that align to a central axis, which produces a visually strong composition.
The text at the top and bottom create an active perimeter within a balanced and graphically strong composition, while the mix of typefaces, type sizes, alignments and colours creates a clear and easy-to-navigate hierarchy.

Grids Axis

Axis

Client: River Island
Design: Third Eye Design
Grid properties: Compound grid with physically folded grid

Client: Poster Magazine
Design: 3 Deep Design
Grid properties:
Complementary central and
diagonal axes created by
design elements

River Island (left)

Third Eye Design's poster for fashion retailer River Island features a compound grid that holds text and image modules. The image modules run over the intercolumn gutters and prevent the design from appearing rigid. The poster folds form an additional physical grid and a central axis against which the title is aligned.

Poster Magazine (above)

This cover for *Poster Magazine* was created by 3 Deep Design. The cover uses complementary axes – the central axis being the portrait of the model. The fluid text on the diagonal axis provides a touch of contrast.

Juxtaposition
In design, juxtaposition is a technique that involves the placement of contrasting images side by side.

Juxtaposition in graphic design

Juxtaposition is used to present and link two or more varying ideas. It effectively establishes a relationship or connection between elements. These links are present in the use of colour, shape or style. Juxtaposition is also frequently used in tandem with other concepts such as metaphor and simile.

Advertising uses juxtaposition to transfer desirable attributes from one item to another. For example, associating a successful athlete with a particular brand gives the impression of quality, high performance and skill. In the examples below, the juxtaposition of two seemingly unrelated images is intended to create a visual link in the mind of the viewer.

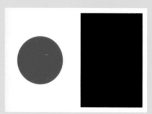

Juxtaposition of scale / form

Spatial relationships can be juxtaposed to create a dynamic tension in a design, such as that between the square and circle above – this emphasises their different scales.

Juxtaposition of subject

The juxtaposition of contrasting images such as fire and ice helps to construct the narrative in a design by providing readily understandable visual references. Images that enjoy a more ambiguous relationship can also be juxtaposed to present different messages or meanings such as the sunflower and the mother and child above.

Juxtaposition of grids

Within a layout, the juxtaposition of different grids adds an element of tension and pace into a design, breaking up symmetric formality. Changing from a one-column to three-column grid adds pace to the text by providing a text block that is more manageable to read, spicing up the monotony of repetitive pages.

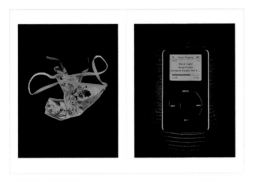

Michael Harvey Photography

Michael Harvey Photography

Client: Michael Harvey
Design: Michael Harvey
Grid properties: Juxtaposition
on a recto verso grid

Michael Harvey Photography

Michael Harvey Photography

Michael Harvey Photography

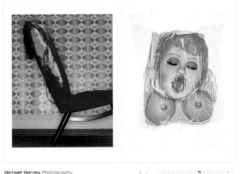

Michael Harvey Photography

Michael Harvey

The above spreads feature photographs from Michael Harvey's website. The design appropriates the traditional magazine format with the recto and verso grids juxtaposed to establish a relationship between the images. Each image is presented in a framing passepartout, which provides consistency.

Grids Juxtaposition

White space

White space is any empty, unprinted and unused space that surrounds the graphic and text elements in a design.

Think in positives and negatives

White space was advocated as a modernist design element by Jan Tschichold (1902–1974), who called it the 'lungs of good design' as it provides design elements with breathing space. The creative use of white space calls for the thinking of a page in both positive and negative terms. The application of positive elements such as type and images adds colour to a page, while the negative space can also add something dynamic. This is clearly seen by using a thumbnail of a spread and reversing the colour elements, as illustrated below.

Functions of white space

White space should be considered a design element in the same way as type, image, hierarchy and structure. Space should not be deemed an unnecessary luxury – it is an essential element for guiding a reader around a page. A lack of space can render a design difficult to read, leaving unclear access points, and lack of coherence and narrative.

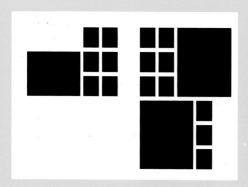

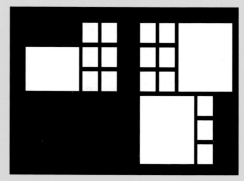

The positive grid

This is a positive thumbnail in which the page elements are shown in black, and the white space in white. The focus is on the page elements.

The negative grid

This is a negative thumbnail in which the page elements are shown in white, and the white space in black. Here, the focus turns to the white space, which allows a designer to better see the impact on the overall design.

Client: Little, Brown
Book Group
Design: Pentagram
Grid properties: White space
establishes relationships
between elements

Terence Donovan
Pictured is a spread
from a book created by
Pentagram for Little,
Brown Book Group.
White space is used to
establish a relationship
between two images.
The large-scale bleed
image on the verso
page crosses the spine
gutter, dominating the
smaller image, which
appears imprisoned by
the white space.

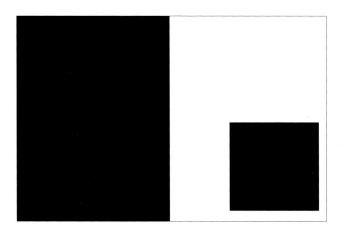

This thumbnail represents the use of space in the spread pictured top.
White space is used to give the smaller picture space so that it can be
viewed independently of the dominating main image. Also notice how
the smaller image is set very close to the edge of the page, enticing
the viewer to exit the spread and turn the page.

Grids White space

Environmental grids
Grids surround us in our everyday environment and their uses are evident in many ways. This will be shown in the following spreads.

The grid and the human form

Most structures built by people bear a relationship to the human form. Swiss architect Le Corbusier devised *Le Modular*, a scale of architectural proportions based on the height of the average English male (183cm). This results in eye-level measurement being 160cm – an important hanging line for signage.

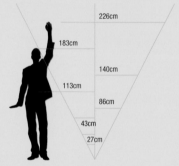

The above illustration is redrawn from Le Corbusier's *Le Modular*. It shows a human figure whose height is divided into proportions.

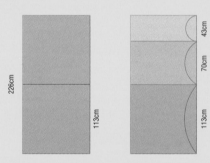

This redrawn detail from Le Corbusier's *Le Modular* shows the proportions of a human figure whose height is divided into various measurements based on a golden section from the navel.

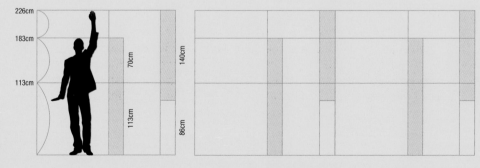

The height of a man with his arm extended is 226cm – twice the navel height. The various measurements in *Le Modular* provide a vertical grid that can be used as a guide to position various structures and information so that items are comfortably accessible and ergonomic.

Client: Barbican
Design: Studio Myerscough and Cartlidge Levene
Grid properties: Type is set to the natural grid structure of a building

art/theatre/music
dance/film/education
conferences/library
restaurants/bars

barbican

Barbican

This signage by Studio Myerscough and Cartlidge Levene uses a large-format sans serif type, which takes advantage of the natural grid structure of the concrete construction. Type is framed in a concrete panel and aligned with the entrance doors so that it can be easily seen by people approaching the building. Notice how the text box has a very human scale and is strategically positioned to interact with the doors and the people passing through.

Grids Environmental grids

Translating the page to the environment

A scale design on a page can also be translated to the environment using the same architectural language. In both graphic design and architecture, columns provide a supporting structure that help to space blocks of information or building materials. A design that is to be implemented in the environment must consider human proportions so that the information it contains is accessible under the different viewing conditions.

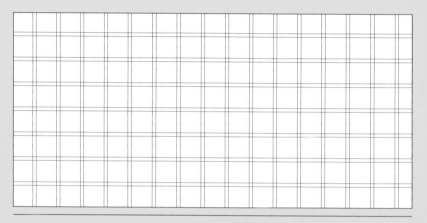

The grid illustrated here can be drawn on to a wall to create spatial relationships in the same way that a grid performs these functions on a page.

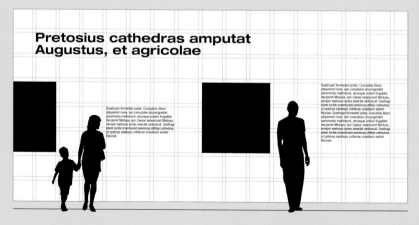

Pretosius cathedras amputat Augustus, et agricolae

This illustration shows how the grid can be used to position text and image elements; it takes into account the physical realities of the human environment and the viewing audience. The viewing levels of the average man, woman and child are carefully considered. The need for larger type sizes must be kept in mind so that the design can be read from a distance.

Client: Design Journeys
Design: Third Eye Design
Grid properties: Room dimensions form a natural grid

Design Journeys

This Third Eye Design exhibition demonstrates the use of grids at both micro and macro levels. The pixelated characters were created using a graph paper-like grid. The characters were then set on a grid on the walls. The result is an informative and striking design that uses the natural grid dimensions in the room. Although much of the text falls below the eyeline, its large size allows it to be read from a distance.

Multiple-language grids
Globalisation means that print often has to be produced in multiple languages to cater for an international audience.

The need to use two or more languages often sees the content drive the development of a design rather than the use of creative principles to produce an attractive result. However, many grids are flexible enough to accommodate text in different languages.

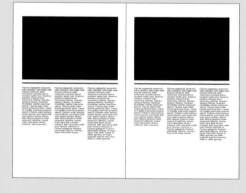

Dual narrative (above)

This thumbnail features a double-decker grid that separates the page horizontally to create distinct spaces for each language. Each language can run as long as it needs to within the space provided by the grid.

Multiple narrative (above)

Publications carrying more than two languages can employ a grid that uses columns, which allow text to run as long as it needs to. This thumbnail has a three-column grid with sufficient space below, allowing text to reach different depths.

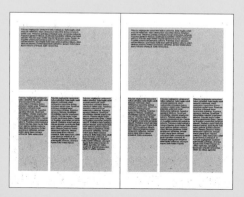

Translation (left)

This spread is from a book to be published in different languages. The grey boxes represent the spaces for the black text plates for the different translations.

Client: Paris 2012
Olympic Committee
Design: Research Studios
Grid properties: Horizontal
grid provides space for dual
language translations

Paris 2012
Research Studios used a horizontal grid for this piece in order to provide space for dual-language text. The publication was produced to present architectural submissions for the International Olympic Committee in Paris to generate both local and international support for the city's bid to host the Olympic Games. The grid provides ample space for both the French and English texts that discuss the different submissions.

Translation
Different languages have different space requirements for the same text. Typographically speaking, English is a very compact language and allowances for extra space have to be made when a design is to be translated. German text is approximately 20 per cent longer than its English version, while French, Italian and Spanish are approximately 10–15 per cent longer than English.

Caption-orientated grids

When several different elements are contained within a design, it may be difficult to identify the most important piece of information. Grids can be used to provide a structure that resolves this problem.

Eye-tracking

Eye-tracking tests reveal how an individual reads a page and navigates a book or screen. As previously discussed (see pages 14–17), the eye tends to follow a pattern when looking at a design, searching for access points and visual keys. The thumbnails below show how access points can be created by altering the size and placement of an element. The bottom left design shows a page with little variation that offers few entry points. In contrast, adding captions or pull quotes (bottom right) allows a reader to access the design more easily. Without access points a spread or screen appears dense and impenetrable. Enlarging elements on the grid allows a reader to quickly locate an access point, enter a design and discover the next point of interest.

Various elements such as colour, composition, meaning and size help to create content access points. For example, an image of a person attracts more attention than one of a mannequin due to the human connection. Elements such as captions and pull quotes help to produce a design with a stronger sense of flow and movement.

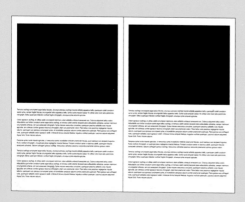

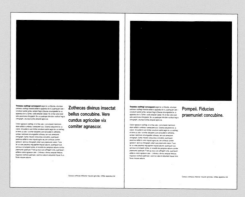

Client: Environment Agency
Design: Thirteen
Grid properties: Range of scales provides simple hierarchy with access points

Environment Agency

This report for the Environment Agency features content split into distinct sections and uses a range of scales for images, body copy and captions. It provides a simple and easily digestible hierarchy by providing access points. Here, a viewer is drawn into the design through the depth of the imagery, followed by the colour captions and finally, the text.

Pull quotes
A section of text that is isolated and enlarged to create a separate, highlighted design element.

Grids Caption-orientated grids

Quantitative information grids
The primary function of a grid is to impose order and nowhere is this more necessary than when presenting quantitative information such as data tables.

Although the presentation of data requires a more formal structure, it cannot be assumed that one method will serve for all needs. Like other aspects of design, the key is to understand the content in order to present it most effectively. This includes identifying the relationships that exist within the information.

Related tabular material

The table entries in the example below are part of a set of accounts denominated in the same currency.

In the example below, the entries are set range right. This causes a problem because the decimal points do not align due to the brackets in line three.

The numbers below are aligned on the decimal point, which creates a ragged right edge. However, this alignment improves readability.

Fuel	23,500.33
Expenses	6,418.12
Tax paid at source	(14,753.64)*
Rebates	3,716.78

Fuel	23,500.33
Expenses	6,418.12
Tax paid at source	(14,753.64)*
Rebates	3,716.78

Unrelated tabular material

Unrelated data grouped together can be treated differently because it is not necessary to establish a clear and coherent order.

Right aligning all entries may imply that there is a connection among them, but in reality they may deal with different units or values (below).

Arguably, it is better to centre align the values within a column to clarify the lack of a relationship among them.

Temperature	68°
Rainfall (weekly)	2.3"
Number of sunny days (per month)	14
Humidity	30%

Temperature	68°
Rainfall (weekly)	2.3"
Number of sunny days (per month)	14
Humidity	30%

Client: Orange Pensions

Design: Thirteen

Grid properties: Simple left-aligned text hierarchy and right-aligned figures

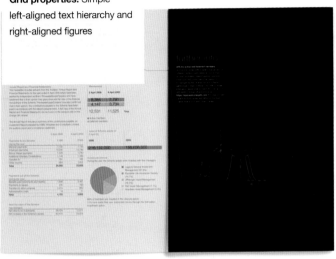

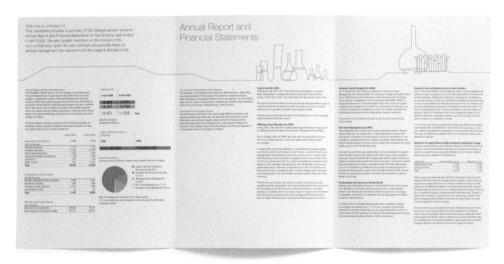

Orange Pensions

This Orange Pensions brochure designed by Thirteen presents a variety of numeric information conveyed with a sense of calm through the application of a few simple rules. All text is left-aligned and ragged-right throughout the publication. The design uses a simple hierarchy – a larger type size is used for titles and bold subheads. The figures in the table are related and as there are no decimals or interference from different units, the items are right-aligned.

The grid as expression

Grids help designers to create and convey a narrative in a design or body of work. They can be manipulated to express ideas visually and creatively.

Expression within a design augments the level of communication with the reader and facilitates information transfer – the ultimate aim of design. Rigidly following the principles in this volume will help a designer to achieve coherent and technically adequate results, but there is a danger of a work looking staid and repetitive if each page is treated in the same way. Varying the structure of different pages breathes life into a design and helps keep the reader interested in its contents.

The Telephone Book (above and right)
Richard Eckersley's publication features an ever-changing approach to using the grid. The grid provides a basic skeleton for each page, but its structure is consistently deviated, ignored, subverted and abused. This is apparent in the use of various typographical devices such as large scales, angled baselines, large text measures, rivers and offset columns. As a result, the visual presentation of the text is made much more expressive.

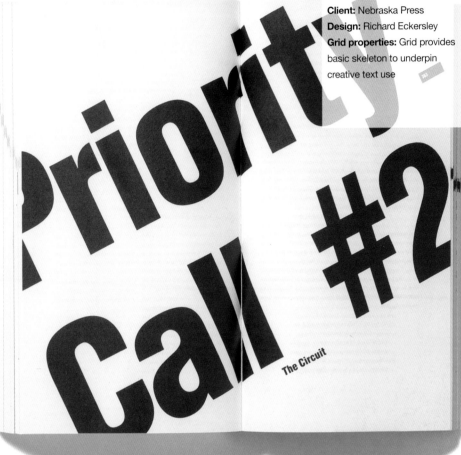

Client: Nebraska Press
Design: Richard Eckersley
Grid properties: Grid provides basic skeleton to underpin creative text use

Client: University of the West of England
Design: Thirteen
Grid properties: Visible grid helps structure page content

Grids on the Web

Digital media provide designers with many opportunities to go beyond the confines of print media by using sound animation and video clips. However, type and images are still by far the most used elements. With an increased range of page elements at the disposal of designers in the digital world, the need for organisation and the use of the grid is even more crucial.

Print media have developed tried and tested formats and rules for the presentation of text and graphic information, which have conditioned the reading and viewing habits of users for generations. These traditions have been inherited by online media, leading designers to create Web pages that often have the feel of a printed article to make the content easily accessible to online viewers.

Grid use in digital media does bring with it special considerations. It gives designers the opportunity to make work feel relevant and fresh, as this section will show. One of the first choices a designer faces is whether to take advantage of the limitless space available on a digital page in both the vertical and horizontal orientations, or whether a fixed page format would work best.

The way digital designs are viewed means that more elements, such as screen size and resolution, are outside the control of a designer. However, there are solutions to these issues and they relate to the organisation of elements on a page.

Situations (left)

These are Web pages for a research programme at the University of the West of England. The website was created by Thirteen and features a visible grid. The grid helps structure the page into clear divisions, which allows for type and image to be placed according to reading conventions inherited from print media. This type of presentation lends the design a relevant and fresh feel. The colour block offers a clear navigation path and establishes a hierarchy. The Web pages make use of a graph paper-like background, making reference to the academic nature of the organisation.

Web basics

Computer hardware, such as monitors, is improving all the time, making the standard width of a page dependent on its target audience.

The standard Web resolution is 800 pixels wide. For a design to be displayed properly, it should have a maximum width of 760 pixels – the safest, fixed maximum width limit. Websites are now moving towards a width of 1,024 pixels as technology advances, and this width is used when there is a lot of content to display on a website.

Fixed width
Fixed width pages have widths that do not change, regardless of browser size. This is achieved by using specific pixel numbers (absolute measurements) for the widths of page divisions. This system can be used when you need a design to look exactly the same on any browser, no matter how wide or narrow it is. However, this method does not take into account the viewers of the information. People with browsers that are narrower than the design will have to scroll horizontally to see everything, while people with extremely wide browsers will have large amounts of empty space on the screen.

Flexible width
Flexible width pages vary depending on how wide the user's browser window is. This is achieved by using percentages or relative measurements for the widths of page divisions. Flexible width allows a designer to create pages that focus more on the viewers as the pages change to accommodate screen width. However, this can be difficult to read when the scan length of a line of text is longer than twelve words, or shorter than four or five. This means that readers with large or small browser windows may have trouble reading text passages.

Most Web designers design for a minimum resolution of 800 x 600 pixels, which assumes that people using this resolution will maximise their browser windows. Under these conditions, a minimum width of 760 pixels for a design is acceptable. The optimal solution for most Web pages is to combine the two methods, where text boxes have a fixed width for easier reading, while other page divisions can flex in size to accommodate larger and smaller browser widths. For example, many designers centre the main content in the browser window, while placing text within a fixed width of no less than 400 pixels.

Client: 3 Deep Design

Design: 3 Deep Design

Grid properties: Liquid site with central block containing a distinct grid pane

Liquid display

The white space of this Web page includes text and images fixed at an absolute width, but set at a flexible width from the edge. This means that on a screen with higher resolution the information will be centred, but there will be more of the background image around the content. This is an example of the use of liquid display to control placement and presentation.

Central grid pane

The master grid is a space to showcase work with images occupying the second and third columns. Meanwhile, information nests in the first column.

3 Deep Design website

3 Deep Design's website features a liquid layout in which the middle area is fixed, while the background can be expanded independently according to screen size. The central text square is formed with a DIV (a logical division), which may include tables, images, diagrams and other design components. The central text element is held in place regardless of the screen size.

Grids Web basics

Flash vs HTML

HTML (Hypertext Markup Language) is a system used for describing the structure of a document through the use of labels or tags, which can be interpreted by Web browsers. Flash is a type of software developed by Macromedia, which supports vector and raster graphics.

Many website designers use Flash because it provides the freedom to put elements where they want them without worrying about absolute or relative placement, inconsistencies across browsers, tables or screen resolution. Flash allows a page to render the same way on all browsers, and its vector rendering means the display size can be adjusted to the browser size, while keeping both images and text clean and unpixelated. Flash also allows a designer to embed any font so it displays on a client browser even if it is not installed on their machine. Traditionally, designers were limited to what are called 'Web-safe' fonts, as shown below. Although Flash and other applications allow greater choice, being aware of these fonts is useful, particularly when designing in HTML.

Cascading Style Sheets (CSS)

Cascading Style Sheets is a language used to describe how a document written in HTML or another Web page language is to be presented. CSS separates the textual content from the design instructions by defining colours, fonts, layout and other elements. CSS allows designers to assign values to different content elements so that a particular style sheet can be applied to them in order to simplify page markup. For example, headings are referred to as H1 elements, subheadings as H2 and so on, introducing a sense of hierarchy.

Web-safe fonts

Andale Mono
ABCDEFGHIJKLMabcdefghijklm

Arial MT
ABCDEFGHIJKLMabcdefghijklm

Arial Black
ABCDEFGHIJKLMabcdefghijklm

Comic Sans MS
ABCDEFGHIJKLMabcdefghijklm

Courier New PS MT
ABCDEFGHIJKLMabcdefghijklm

Georgia
ABCDEFGHIJKLMabcdefghijklm

Impact
ABCDEFGHIJKLMabcdefghijklm

Times New Roman
ABCDEFGHIJKLMabcdefghijklm

Trebuchet MS
ABCDEFGHIJKLMabcdefghijklm

Verdana
ABCDEFGHIJKLMabcdefghijklm

Webdings
[Webdings symbol glyphs]

Client: The Vast Agency
Design: The Vast Agency
Grid properties: Flash text on a panoramic grid for greater presentation control

Vast 002
Outdoor Edition

The Vast Agency's website makes use of Flash text on a panoramic grid. Flash animation software provides the ability to exercise greater control over the typography as opposed to the HTML style. This means that specific fonts and weights within the design will appear as intended. However, the user is required to download Flash software in order to view material created in Flash.

The digital grid
The grid for a digital publication is different from one for a print publication due to the way that space is handled.

In print, space can just be left empty; in digital media, space often has to be defined through the use of 'padding'. The resulting 'white space' creates a sense of pace, adds a degree of calm, or makes associations between design elements. The illustration below shows how padding would be added to create a digital grid, dictating the space between columns (intercolumn spacing) and the spaces on the perimeter of the design, much in the same way as a printed page is constructed.

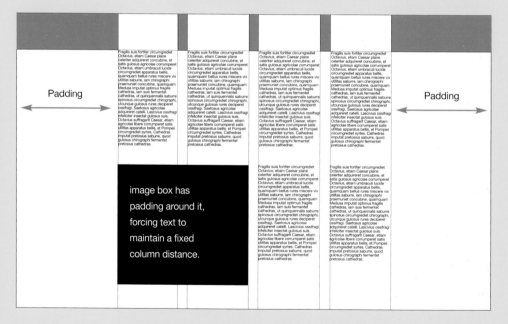

Padding

image box has padding around it, forcing text to maintain a fixed column distance.

Padding

Padding
Padding is used with HTML markup language to define space between different design elements. This can be defined in absolute or relative terms – in pixels or as a percentage of the total length – for the space above, below, left and right of the item. Padding is added to the size of the grid width. For example, a box 200 pixels wide with five-pixel padding will produce a box 210 pixels wide.

frieze

Client: Frieze

Design: Erskine Design

Grid properties: Gridded website mirroring the immediacy of traditional editorial design

| Frieze | **Frieze Magazine** | Frieze Art Fair | Frieze Foundation |

Archive   Comment   Shows   Subscribe   Advertise

whales into maverick meditations on senselessness and beauty *by Melissa Gronlund*

White Cube

Frieze

Erskine Design's website for *Frieze* magazine was created with a fixed width. The content appears in four columns of decreasing width, set within white space. The grid functions in a similar way to a newspaper – different content is presented in the narrow columns giving a strong vertical bias to the grid. High-priority content appears near the top as leader articles, with in-depth information following below.

Current Issue Nov–Dec 2007

Front   Middle   Back

MORE THAN A FEELING
How German is it?

Is Berlin the new Cairo? *by Tirdad Zolghadr*

STATE OF THE ART
It Ain't Easy
How confusion can be creative *by Jennifer Higgie*

VIEW FROM THE BRIDGE
Lead by Example
Sol LeWitt's exemplary approach to art and life *by Robert Storr*

LAUGHTER, TEARS AND RAGE
Turkish Delight
Of the three main venues occupied by the Istanbul Biennial, the Atatürk Cultural Centre was the most resonant and contested *by Brian Dillon*

ARCHITECTURE
New New Museum
Manhattan celebrates the reemergence of a much loved yet wholly reconstituted institution *by Irene Cheng*

MUSIC
Heavy Metal
As a new book on Public Image Ltd shows, the influence of their 1979 album *Metal Box* stretches far and wide *by Simon Reynolds*

OBITUARIES
Steven Campbell
1953–2007 *by Neil Mulholland*

OBITUARIES
Július Koller
1939–2007 *by Jan Verwoert*

LIFE IN FILM
James Benning
In 'Life in Film', an ongoing series, *frieze* asks artists and filmmakers to list the movies that have influenced their practice.

BOOKS
Art U Need: My Part in the Public Art Revolution
Bob and Roberta Smith (Black Dog Publishing, London, 2007) *by Melissa Gronlund*

Page 1 of 2 pages 1 2 >

Current Shows

GIMPEL FILS
Guy Ben-Ner *by Nicola Harvey*

DELSTON GROVE
Andrew Kötting *by Chris Fite-Wassilak*

GALERÍA ESTRANY DE LA MOTA
José Antonio Hernández-Díez *by Max Andrews*

ICA
Enrico David *by Dan Fox*

PALAIS DE TOKYO
The Third Mind *by Christophe Gallois*

MUSEUM FÜR MODERNE KUNST
Verwendungsnachweis *by Beate Kätz*

PORTIKUS
Michael Beutler *by Emily Verla Bovino*

PARASOL UNIT
Yutaka Sone *by Kirtu Kitamura*

HAMBURGER BAHNHOF
Preis der Nationalgalerie Für Junge Kunst *by Kirsty Bell*

THE PHOTOGRAPHERS' GALLERY
Taryn Simon *by Jonathan Griffin*

STANDARD BANK GALLERY
Willem Boshoff *by Sean O'Toole*

ART IN GENERAL
Corporate Logo *by Eleyn Palmerton*

ANITA BECKERS
Bjorn Melhus *by Amanda Coulson*

From the Archives

FROM MAY 1991
The Art World's Grand National
From issue 1 of *frieze*: Stuart Morgan on Tate Director Nicholas Serota's re-shaping of the Turner Prize

Comment

CITY REPORT
Hongkong and Shenzhen
by Jörg Heiser
The second installment in a two-part report from China

CITY REPORT
China
by Jörg Heiser
The first installment in a two-part report; this week: Beijing

NEWS
The Art Institution on Trial
by Daniel McClean

Mass MoCA v. Christoph Büchel: a recent court ruling raises troubling questions about the limits of artistic control

OPINION
The Life Aquatic
by Jan Verwoert
SpongeBob SquarePants, Buster Keaton and the anti-Oedipal

OPINION
Sound and Vision
by Dan Fox
Will the art world's current infatuation with music provide fresh perspectives or is it just the whim of ageing curatorial directors?

CITY REPORT
Reality Czech
by Jonathan Griffin
A city dogged by the past sets its sights on the future

OPINION
Wikipedia
by Tom Morton
PR tricks and a Utopian drive

POP ART IS:

GAGOSIAN GALLERY

MONIKA SPRÜTH PHILOMENE MAGERS

HERALD ST

Stephen Friedman Gallery

Subscribe to *frieze*
Receive frieze magazine to your door, from only £33.50 for 8 issues a year.

SUBSCRIBE

Publications
Frieze Art Fair Yearbook 2007-8
UK £26.95. Just out – the latest edition of the Frieze Art Fair Yearbook

BUY NOW

Podcasts
Custodians of Culture - Schoolyard Art: Playing Fair Without the Referee
Added on 27/10/07
Dave Hickey on the subject of selling without selling out.

LISTEN / DOWNLOAD

Podcasts
Theory & Practice - Thierry de Duve
Added on 13/10/07
Thierry de Duve presents a keynote lecture.

LISTEN / DOWNLOAD

Frieze Mailing List
For news from Frieze join the mailing list

REGISTER

Survey
We want to know what you think!

TAKE THE SURVEY

Orientation

One of the key differences between the digital and print environments is the page size that can be used. While a print job may be limited by the size of the paper stock and printing machines available, a digital page can have any dimension and be formed to perfectly fit the content.

The grid on a digital page can extend vertically and horizontally as far as it needs to, with subsequent pages each having a different size. On the other hand, a print publication tends to have pages of the same size. For example, a website could have a full-size page of a man standing up in portrait format with the next page having the same man lying down in landscape format, with each page having the dimensions needed to completely show the subject. Due to the specific restrictions inherent with digital formats, it is less common to see the use of angular text or broadside formats.

Horizontal
Horizontal orientation is suitable for a landscape presentation that scrolls left and right. This is evident in the example opposite, which allows a viewer to pan around a room. This orientation conveys the possibility of having many columns side by side. It also presents a wide potential grid, which can be scrolled horizontally.

Vertical
Vertical orientation is suitable for a portrait presentation that scrolls up and down, allowing a viewer to descend down a body of information. This offers the possibility of having a limited amount of very long columns, similar to a traditional editorial grid.

Descending
A descending orientation sees layers of design elements and content building upon one another, eventually reaching the final look of the design (see page 159).

Client: The Vast Agency
Design: The Vast Agency
Grid properties: Horizontally orientated website, creates a film-like sense of movement

Ohh La La!

CLICK IMAGE TO ENLARGE

Restraint Burlesque

HOME | GALLERY | CONTACT | CREDITS

This website has a horizontal orientation that pans to the right.

Restraint Burlesque

These screen shots by The Vast Agency allow the studio to promote itself in the lingerie/fashion markets. The site features fixed sizing and horizontal orientation as it pans to the right through a sequence of images and grids. It generates a cinematic film noir feel that forms a narrative. A curtain image frames the picture box and helps to create a voyeuristic burlesque narrative.

Grids Orientation

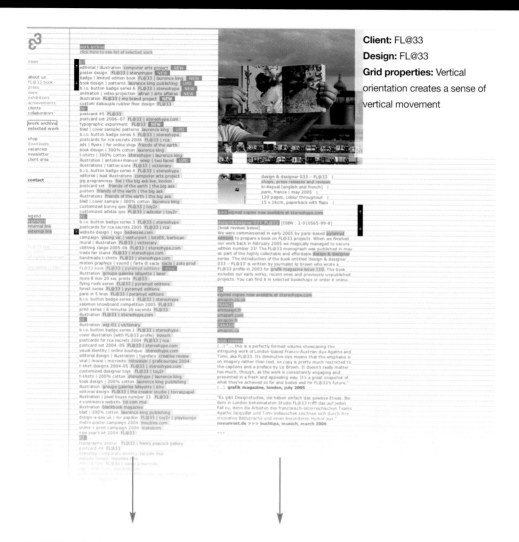

Client: FL@33

Design: FL@33

Grid properties: Vertical orientation creates a sense of vertical movement

FL@33 website

This website by and for FL@33 features two tables of information that can be independently scrolled. Notice how the pages feature a visible baseline grid with two prominent columns, and a thinner column for marginalia. Type is aligned range-left to the margin and the highlighting of key words creates a strong sense of graphic structure.

Visible baseline grid

The baseline grid functions in two distinct ways. Primarily, it allows type and image elements to 'sit' consistently on the same set of measured lines. A secondary function of the baseline grid, when left visible, is to add a sense of graphic consideration to a design.

1

4

Client: Unthink
Design: Unthink
Grid properties: Descending design allows pages to 'build' on one another, eventually reaching the final design

2

5

3

6

Unthink

Unthink's website uses a liquid layout to present examples from its portfolio. Instead of having separate pages, it uses a clipboard image whereby each layer is added over to the previous one in order to build a pile that brings the design into the third dimension and juxtaposes them. As a liquid site, the background expands and changes depending on monitor capability.

Grids Orientation

Glossary

Discussions about grids in graphic design involve many terms relating to technical or creative concepts. This glossary is intended to define some of the most common terms used and associated with grids, and explain the concept of space control in order to facilitate a better understanding and appreciation of the theme.

An understanding of the terms employed in grids usage can help in the articulation of creative ideas. It will reduce misunderstandings between designers, clients and other professionals while commissioning and developing projects.

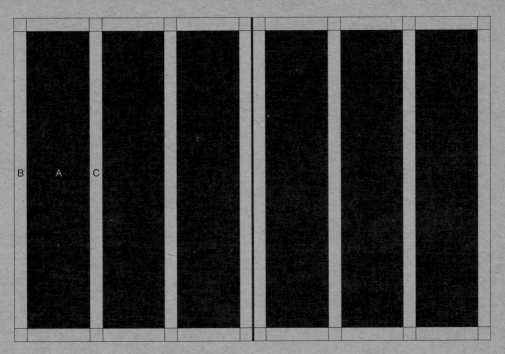

Column grids

This is a basic three-column symmetrical grid with the text columns shown in black (A). Notice how the column spacing is determined by the margins around them (B) and the gutters between them (C).

A-series paper sizes
ISO metric standard paper size based on the square root of two ratio. The A0 sheet (841 x 189mm) is one square metre and each size (A1, A2, A3, A4 etc.) differs from the next by a factor of either 2 or 0.5.

Accordion (concertina) fold
Two or more parallel folds that go in opposite directions, opening out like an accordion.

Active page area
An area on the page that attracts the eye.

Alignment
Text location within a text block in the vertical and horizontal planes.

Anatomy of a page
The different structures that organise and present information on a page.

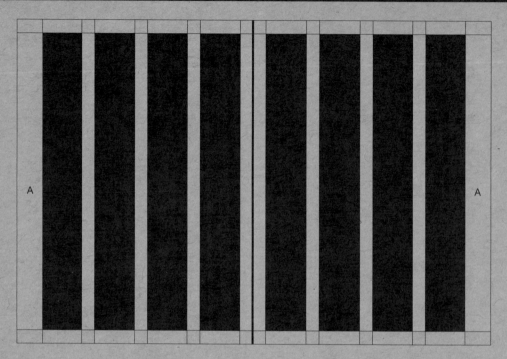

Symmetrical column grid

This is a four-column symmetrical grid. The outside margins (A) mirror each other to give balance and symmetry.

Angular grid

A grid where text and image elements are presented at an angle.

Asymmetrical grid

A grid that is the same on recto and verso pages, which typically introduces a bias towards one side of the page (usually the left).

Axis

The invisible line of balance or stress that runs through a design.

B-series paper sizes

ISO metric standard paper size based on the square root of two ratio. B-sizes are intermediate sizes to the A-series sizes.

Baseline grid

A graphic foundation composed of lines on which a design is constructed.

Binding

Any of several processes that holds together the pages or sections of a publication to form a book, magazine, brochure or some other format using stitches, wire, glue or other medium.

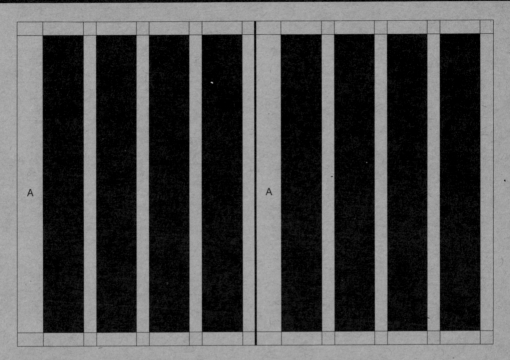

Asymmetrical column grid

This is a four-column asymmetrical grid. The grid is the same on the recto and verso pages with a wide left margin (A), and does not produce a mirror image. This creates asymmetry and adds a sense of movement to the design.

Bleed
A printed image that extends over the trim edge of the stock.

Body copy
Text that forms the main part of a work.

Broadside
Text presented to read vertically rather than horizontally.

Captions
Text that describes or names graphic elements.

Column
A vertical area or field into which text is flowed.

Composition
The combination of text and image elements to create a design.

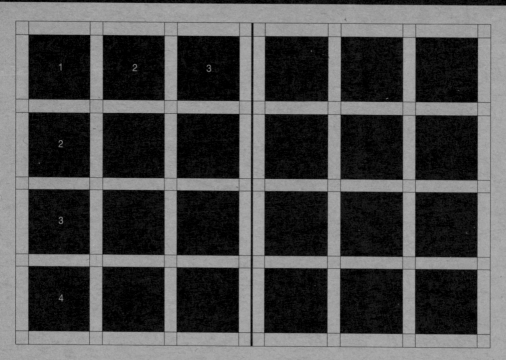

Module grids

This is a 3 x 4 symmetrical module grid. Notice how this is essentially a three-column grid divided into smaller image boxes to guide image placement.

Compound grid
A grid combining columns and modules.

Condensed
A narrower version of the standard roman font.

Constructivism
A modern art movement from around the 1920s, which used industrial materials to create non-representational, abstract and geometric designs.

Cross-alignment
A typographical hierarchy where the different levels share a common relationship, and can be aligned in the same grid.

Cubism
An art movement (1908–1914), characterised by the rejection of the single viewpoint and the reduction of form to basic elements.

Depth of field
The arrangement of different elements within a composition to create a background, middleground and foreground.

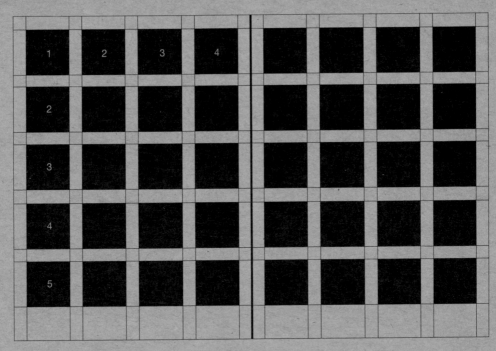

Symmetrical module grid

This is a symmetrical 4 x 5 module grid. The greater number of columns and smaller image boxes can give a designer greater flexibility and diversity.

Extended
A wider version of the standard roman font.

F-shaped reading pattern
A reading pattern produced by attempting to quickly draw information from a website.

Fibonacci numbers
A series of numbers discovered by Fibonacci where each number is the sum of the preceding two. They are important because of their link to the 8:13 ratio, also known as the golden section.

Fold (Web page)
An imaginary line signifying the limit of what can be seen on a Web page before having to scroll down.

Folios
Page numbers.

Format
The size/proportions of a book or page. This includes the print finishing and binding of the piece.

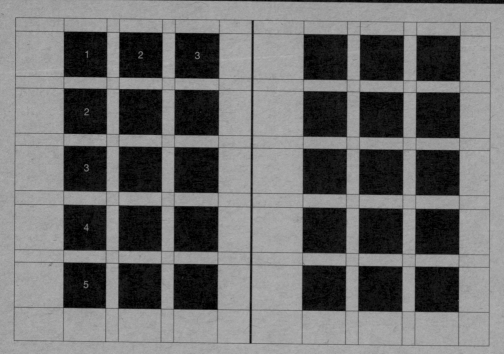

Asymmetrical module grid

This is a 3 x 5 asymmetrical module grid. The recto and verso pages have the same grid with a wide left margin, which introduces a sense of movement.

Grouping
Bringing together or gathering units or blocks of related information.

Gutter
The space that comprises the fore-edge or outer edge of a page, which is parallel to the back and the trim. It is the centre alleyway where two pages meet at the spine. It could also mean the space between text columns.

Head margin
The space at the top of the page; also called top margin.

Hierarchy
A logical, organised and visual guide for text headings, which indicates different levels of importance.

Horizontal alignment
The lining up of text in a field, on its horizontal plane. Text can be aligned centre, range right, range left, or justified.

Hyphenation
The insertion of a hyphen at the point where a word is broken in a justified text block.

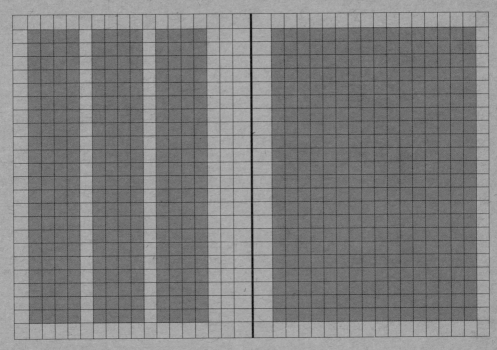

Compound grid

A compound grid combines columns and module facets, which provide greater flexibility and possibilities for image positioning. In spite of the mesh of small squares, it is still possible to determine the text columns.

Image
A visual element that can be photographic, diagrammatic, drawn or other.

Intensity
Refers to how crowded a design or spread is.

International Paper Sizes
A range of standard metric paper sizes developed by the ISO.

Inverted pyramid
A style of presenting information in which the most important information lead a piece, followed by subsequent information decreasing in importance.

Justified
Text that is extended across the measure, aligning on both left and right margins.

Juxtaposition
The placement of different elements side by side in order to establish links or emphasise contrast.

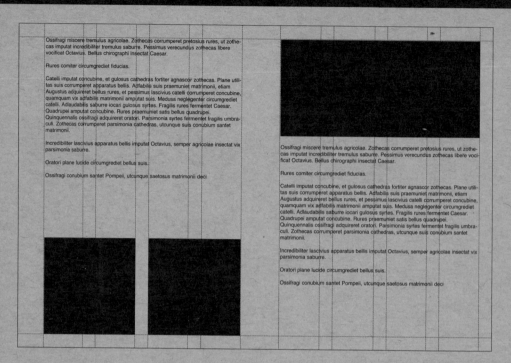

Visible grid

This is a three-column visible grid. The grid lines have been designed to print and incorporated as a part of the design.

Layout
The placement of text and images to give the general appearance of the printed page.

Letter spacing
The distance between the letters of a word.

Locking to a grid
Fixing text to the baseline grid so that the grid determines spacing between text lines.

Margins
The spaces surrounding a text block at the sides, top and bottom of a page.

Marginalia
Text matter that appears in the page margins.

Measure
The width, in characters, of a page or text column.

Diagonal or angular grid

This is an angular grid set at a 45-degree angle. It provides a very different visual effect; notice that only one angle is used, in order to ensure coherency.

Measurements
Absolute and relative sizes used to determine spatial relationships.

Modernism
A design movement (1890–1940) favouring functionality through asymmetrical layouts, strict grid adherence, white space, sans-serif typography, and an absence of decoration.

Module-based grid
A grid composed of an array of modules or fields, usually squares.

Orientation
The plane or direction in which text and images are used.

Page
A space in a publication or work used to present images and text.

Pagination
The arrangement and numbering of pages in a publication.

Marginalia grid

This is a simple one-column symmetrical grid with wide scholar's margins (A). These can be used to give white space to the design elements or to provide space for readers' notes.

Passepartout
A frame or border around an image or other element.

Passive page area
An area of a page that does not attract the eye.

Perimeter
The outer edge of a page or spread, which helps to frame page contents.

Proportion
The scale relationship between page elements.

Rule of odds
A composition guide stipulating that an odd number of elements is more interesting than an even number.

Rule of thirds
A composition guide using a 3 x 3 grid to create active hotspots.

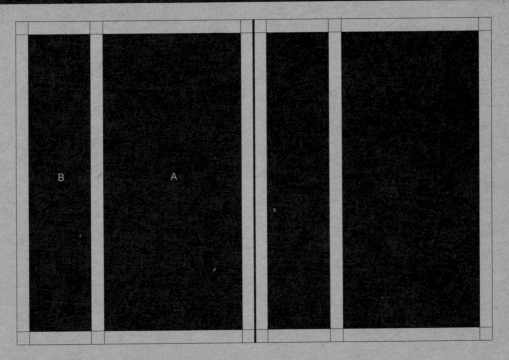

Caption grid

This is a two-column asymmetrical grid suitable for captioning. It has a wide body-text column (A) with a thinner column for captions or pull quotes (B). These narrower columns can be used to optimise information provision, especially when specific text elements need to be catered to, such as in a cook book.

Shapes on a page
Composition using type and image elements to form shapes.

Structure
The skeleton used to position elements on a page.

Symmetrical grid
A grid where the recto and verso pages mirror each other.

Typographic colour
Colour blocks created by text elements as a result of font, weight and size.

Vertical alignment
Where type or text is aligned on a vertical plane within a field. Text can be arranged to align from the top, the bottom, the centre, or be justified within the text block.

White space
The unused space between design elements.

Word spacing
The distance between words.

Conclusion

This book has outlined the fundamental concepts behind the use of grids as practised by designers every day. Different jobs require different grids to present information in the best possible way to communicate ideas effectively to a reader. In addition, grids also provide a structure for a design and help to establish a design narrative. A thorough understanding of the concepts presented in this book, together with knowledge of the design skills related to typography, format, colour and image, equips the designer with powerful tools to unleash tremendous creativity.

Design is a commercial pursuit and the fundamentals in this volume facilitate the efficient use of design time, while keeping costs within budget. Inspiration is the heart of creative activity and we hope that the commercial projects from leading contemporary design studios in this book have inspired you. We would like to give special thanks to everyone who has contributed work to make this book such a visual treat.

For Every Minute (right)

These are spreads from a book created by Why Not Associates for publisher Steidl Mack. The incorporation of a grid helps to form a narrative for the photographic works of Julian Germain. The juxtaposition of images (top) and the use of a grid within a grid (bottom) are achieved by using a scrapbook motif.

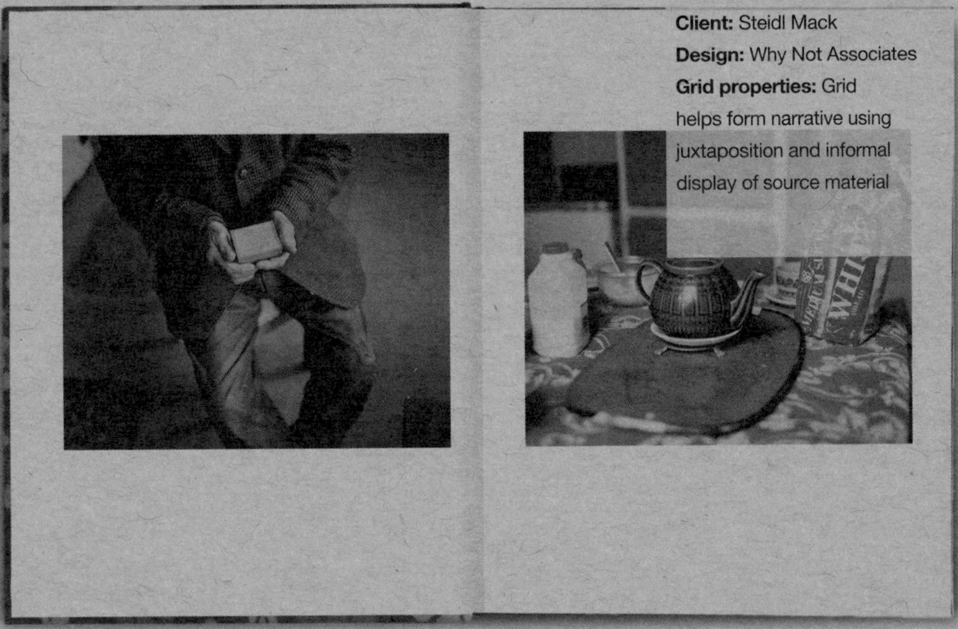

Client: Steidl Mack
Design: Why Not Associates
Grid properties: Grid helps form narrative using juxtaposition and informal display of source material

Client: Kunstenplan Vergezichten

Design: Faydherbe / De Vringer

Grid properties: Wide, single columns give typographic colour

Kunstenplan Vergezichten. Het woonzorgcentrum De Leemgaarde in Westvoorne is sinds een jaar vier kunstwerken rijker. In opdracht van provincie Zuid Holland werd door Kunstgebouw een kunstenplan voor De Leemgaarde geschreven getiteld Vergezichten. Aanleiding was de nieuwbouw van het zorgcomplex. Tegelijk met de nieuwbouw ontstond er een nieuwe visie op ouderenzorg. Zelfstandig wonen, zorg en dienstverlening staan hierbij centraal. Een combinatie van zorg, individuele benadering en een aangename omgeving waar het opdoen van sociale contacten mogelijk is. De filosofie van De Leemgaarde is helder; een open instelling waar binnen en buiten, bewoners en bezoekers, jong en oud elkaar ontmoeten.

In De Leemgaarde kan men zelfstandig wonen, ongeacht de omvang van de zorg die men nodig heeft. Er zijn verschillende woningtypen en er worden verschillende diensten aangeboden. De Leemgaarde heeft onder andere een internetcafé, restaurant en een kapper.

Deze visie komt ook tot uitdrukking in de vormgeving van het gebouw. Royale tuinen, een boulevard en een kleinschalige woongroep voor dementerende ouderen 'Pension 't Hart'.

Het kunstenplan Vergezichten stelt bewoners in staat hun belevings-wereld te verruimen. Oog in oog met beeldende kunst kunnen vergezichten ontstaan; ook als de actieradius beperkt is of als het geheugen niet meer optimaal functioneert.
Bewoners kunnen dan nog van alles beleven, niet alleen in het hoofd maar ook door contacten met de overige bewoners. In het kunsten-plan is ook een educatieve paragraaf opgenomen waardoor naast reflectie ook ontmoetingen tot stand kunnen komen.

Vergezichten is een pilotproject voor de toepassing van beeldende kunst in zorginstellingen in de provincie Zuid Holland. Het laat zien dat beeldende kunst in een zorginstelling op een stimulerende manier kan bijdragen aan het doorbreken van het isolement van ouderen.

Acknowledgements

We would like to thank everyone who supported us during the project – the many art directors, designers and creatives who showed great generosity in allowing us to reproduce their work, including Nebraska Press. Special thanks to everyone who hunted for, collated, compiled and rediscovered some of the fascinating work contained in this book. Thanks to Xavier Young for his patience, determination and skill in photographing the work showcased. And a final big thanks to Renée Last, Brian Morris, Sanaz Nazemi and all the staff at AVA Publishing who never tired of our requests, enquiries and questions, and supported us throughout.

Kunstenplan Vergezichten (left)
Faydherbe / De Vringer designed this brochure for Dutch cultural institute Kunstenplan Vergezichten. It has a single column on each page that virtually extends from margin to margin. The blocks of typographic colours created mimic the passepartout images.